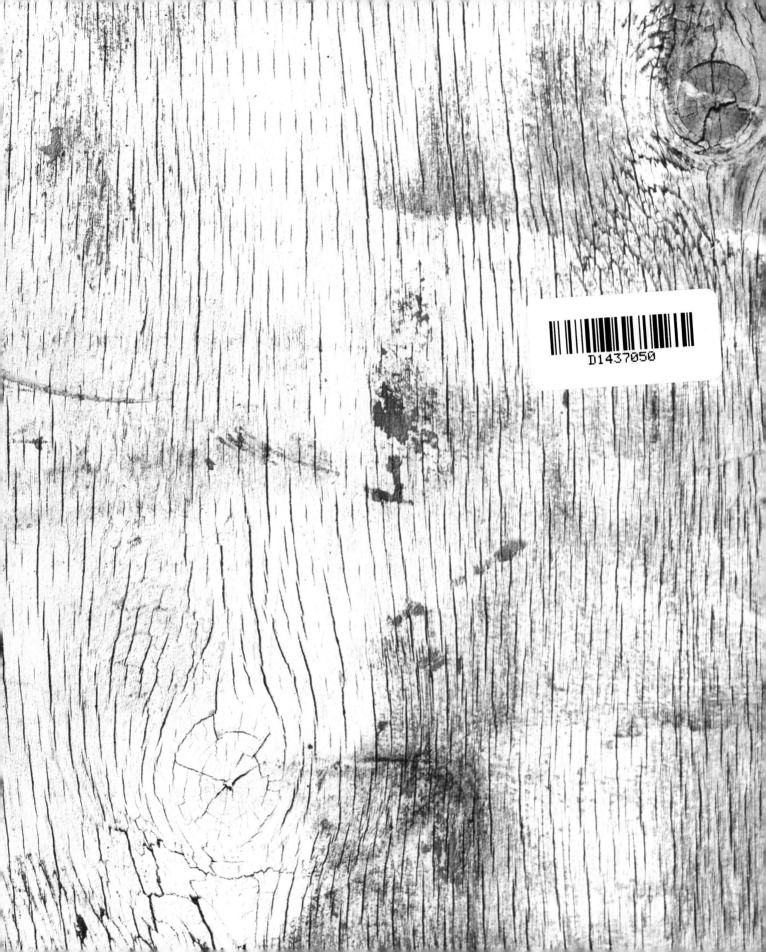

Almost VEGETARIAN

TRIPLE TESTED

Almost VEGETARIAN

Delicious recipes for plant-based meals

TRIPLE TESTED

CONTENTS

Less meat
MORE VEG

People choose to follow a vegetarian diet for ethical, health, or myriad other reasons. And within the world of vegetarianism are various subgroups. The most common group is the lacto-ovo vegetarian who eats dairy products and eggs. There are also lacto-vegetarians who eat dairy but not eggs, and ovo-vegetarians who eat eggs but not dairy. Vegans are the strictest of vegetarians, abstaining from all animal products, including dairy, eggs and even honey. There is, however, a new group of flexible vegetarians (flexitarian), who do eat some white meat, or fish (pescetarian, or as we've affectionately named, "vege-quarian"), and yet still identify themselves as vegetarian.

Why be a vegetarian?

The natural world of plants and seeds offers infinite variety and leaves a lighter footprint on our planet. Those on a vegetarian and vegan diet also tend to weigh less than their meat-eating counterparts and are at a lower risk of developing type-2 diabetes, heart disease, and some cancers. This is because a well-balanced vegetarian diet includes a wide array of plant matter and fiber and tends to be low fat. As with any diet however, it is possible to make it unbalanced by eating too much dairy, fatty, or high sugar foods.

For a well-balanced vegetarian diet, be sure to include a wide range of colorful vegetables, legumes, seeds, and nuts (and dairy if you can):

Calcium is plentiful in dairy products; to compensate, vegans need to include plenty of dark green leafy vegetables (swiss chard, kale, watercress, etc), soy products (tofu and soy milk), sesame seeds, and calcium-enriched cereals.

Vitamin B12 is required for the development of healthy blood cells and the prevention of anemia; since the only food source is meat, non-meat eaters need to either find foods that are fortified with it or take a supplement.

Iron is more readily absorbed from meat sources than plant ones. Since plant sources are not as bioavailable, vegetarians need to eat double to compensate. Good sources are leafy green vegetables, pulses, dried fruit, whole grains, and fortified cereals. Absorption from iron-rich plant sources can be increased further by eating food that is rich in vitamin C, such as citrus, strawberries, tomato, and kale at the same meal.

Zinc is another nutrient that, like iron, isn't absorbed quite as well from plant sources as from meat and seafood. Vegetarians should include whole grains, nuts, pepitas, soy and wheat germ in their diet.

Protein needs are easily met in a vegetarian diet that includes plenty of nuts, legumes, seeds, and whole grains.

Omega-3 fatty acids are readily available from fish and eggs; alternative sources are flax, chia, pepitas, and walnuts.

Iodine is needed for healthy thyroid function, which in turn aids metabolism. For those who omit seafood from their diet, meeting this need can be a challenge, especially since certain vegetables contain a compound that can thwart absorption. Sea vegetables such as nori, wakame, or kombu are good sources, or use a little iodized salt, to meet your requirements.

THE NATURAL WORLD OF PLANTS AND SEEDS OFFERS INFINITE VARIETY AND LEAVES A LIGHTER FOOTPRINT ON OUR PLANET.

Making the switch

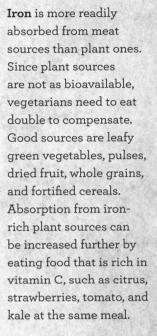

As with anything new, allowing for a period of transition will increase your chances of making a lasting change. With this in mind, the recipes in the Almost Vegetarian chapter contain a little white meat but the real stars are vegetables and whole grains or legumes. Similarly, Everyday Vege-quarian includes a little fish or seafood in their plant-based recipes. Meatless Mondays are full of substantial vegetarian (lacto-ovo) meals created for meat-eaters to try one day a week, while Everyday Vegetarian is a chapter of no-fuss meatless recipes with dairy and eggs that you can enjoy every day of the week. And if you've already made the leap to a completely meat-free, dairy-free, and egg-free diet, then Everyday Vegan is for you, which also includes some sweet treats.

Almost
VEGETARIAN

For the meat eater who would like to add more plant foods to their diet. These recipes contain lots of veggies and some white meat.

Brown rice congee
WITH FRIED GARLIC

PREP + COOK TIME 2 HOURS 25 MINUTES **SERVES** 6

Frying garlic tempers the flavor, bringing out a natural sweetness. Just be careful to fry it quickly, as overcooking will make it bitter.

6 cloves garlic

7 cups water

2 cups vegetable or chicken stock

1½ cups brown rice

2 tablespoons finely chopped ginger

4 green onions, sliced thinly

⅓ pound chicken breast fillet

½ cup vegetable oil

2 tablespoons tamari

½ cup fresh cilantro leaves

2 teaspoons toasted sesame seeds

1 Finely chop 1 garlic clove; thinly slice remaining cloves.
2 Place the water, stock, rice, chopped garlic, ginger, and a quarter of the green onion in a large saucepan; bring to a boil. Add chicken; return to a boil. Reduce heat; simmer, partially covered, for 12 minutes or until chicken is cooked through. Remove chicken from broth mixture; cool for 10 minutes. Shred chicken coarsely.
3 Return broth mixture to a boil. Reduce heat; simmer, partially covered, for 1½ hours or until rice breaks down and forms a thick porridge consistency.
4 Meanwhile, heat oil in a small saucepan over medium heat; cook sliced garlic for 1 minute or until golden. Remove garlic with a slotted spoon; drain on paper towels. Reserve garlic-infused oil.
5 Add chicken and tamari to broth mixture; stir over heat until hot. Serve congee topped with fried garlic, cilantro, sesame seeds, and remaining green onion. Drizzle with reserved garlic-infused oil.

serving suggestion Serve with steamed Asian greens.

VEG IT UP!
LEAVE OUT THE
CHICKEN AND ADD
SOME TOFU.

Kale CAESAR SALAD

PREP + COOK TIME 45 MINUTES (+ COOLING) SERVES 4

Dark leafy greens such as kale provide a rich supply of A and C vitamins, fiber, and phytonutrients that may be useful to prevent heart disease and cancer.

4 cups water

4 sprigs fresh thyme

2 cloves garlic, crushed

½ medium lemon, sliced thinly

¾ pound chicken breast fillets

12 thin slices sourdough baguette

¾ cup finely grated parmesan

1 tablespoon olive oil

8 slices bacon

1 teaspoon white vinegar

4 eggs

½ pound baby kale leaves

GREEN GODDESS DRESSING

¼ cup mayonnaise

2 tablespoons sour cream

¼ cup coarsely chopped fresh flat-leaf parsley

1 tablespoon coarsely chopped fresh basil

1 tablespoon coarsely chopped fresh chives

2 tablespoons water

1 tablespoon lemon juice

1 drained anchovy fillet, chopped coarsely

1 clove garlic, chopped finely

1 Bring the water, thyme sprigs, garlic, and lemon to a boil in a medium saucepan. Add chicken, return to a boil. Reduce heat; simmer, uncovered, for 12 minutes or until chicken is cooked through. Remove chicken; cool 10 minutes, then shred coarsely. Reserve poaching liquid for another use (see tips).

2 Meanwhile, make Green Goddess Dressing.

3 Preheat broiler. Toast bread on one side, then turn and sprinkle with half the parmesan; grill croutons until parmesan melts and is browned lightly.

4 Heat oil in a small frying pan over medium heat, cook bacon until golden and crisp; drain on paper towels.

5 Half fill a large saucepan with water; bring to a boil. Add vinegar to water. Break one 1 egg into a cup then slide into pan; repeat with remaining eggs. When eggs are in pan, return to a boil. Cover pan, turn off heat; let stand 3 minutes or until a light film of egg white sets over the yolks.

6 Meanwhile, place kale and one-quarter of the dressing in a large bowl; toss to combine. Let stand for 5 minutes to soften slightly.

7 Add croutons, bacon, remaining parmesan and dressing; toss to combine. Serve salad topped with poached egg.

green goddess dressing Process ingredients until smooth and combined; season to taste. (Makes ¾ cup)

tips The poaching liquid in step 1 can be used as a light chicken stock for any other recipe in this chapter. Allow to cool; refrigerate and use within 2 days, or freeze for up to 1 month. Don't forget—you can also save the parmesan rind for another use; see page 16.

Chicken schnitzel buns
WITH APPLE SLAW

PREP + COOK TIME 45 MINUTES MAKES 6

½ pound stale sourdough bread, torn coarsely

6 thin chicken schnitzels

½ cup all-purpose flour

2 eggs, beaten lightly

2 tablespoons olive oil

¼ cup butter, chopped coarsely

6 brioche buns

¼ cup aïoli

APPLE SLAW

¼ cup buttermilk

1 tablespoon olive oil

2 teaspoon dijon mustard

1 tablespoon lemon juice

1 teaspoon caraway seeds, toasted, crushed coarsely

2 cups shredded purple cabbage

½ red apple, cut into matchsticks

½ baby fennel bulb, sliced thinly, reserve fronds

1 cup fresh flat-leaf parsley leaves, torn

1 Make Apple Slaw.

2 Process sourdough until fine crumbs form. Transfer to a baking sheet. Coat chicken in flour; shake away excess. Dip chicken in egg mixture, then coat in bread crumbs.

3 Preheat oven to 250°F. Line a baking sheet with parchment paper.

4 Heat half the oil and half the butter in a large frying pan over medium-high; cook chicken for 2 minutes each side or until golden and cooked through. Transfer to baking sheet; keep warm in oven. Repeat with remaining oil, butter, and schnitzels. Halve schnitzels.

5 Split buns in half. Spread bun bases with aïoli; top with schnitzel halves, apple slaw, and bun tops.

apple slaw Combine buttermilk, oil, mustard, and juice in a large bowl; season to taste. Add seeds, cabbage, apple, fennel, reserved fronds, and parsley; toss to combine.

tips We used pink lady apples in this recipe, or you could use a green variety. You could also use panko (Japanese) bread crumbs instead of making your own.

VEG IT UP!
SWAP CHICKEN SCHNITZELS FOR THICKLY SLICED EGGPLANT.

Don't THROW away

TOPS OF LEEKS Save the trimmed green tops of leeks to use in stocks.
TOPS OF GREEN ONION The green part can be used in the same way as the white part, and adds extra color.
STALKS OF SOFT LEAFY HERBS (PARSLEY, CILANTRO) Are just as edible as the leaves; trim and discard the last 1-inch from the ends before using.
STALKS OF WOODY HERBS (ROSEMARY, THYME) Tie them together with kitchen string (to make it easier to retrieve later), and add to homemade tomato sauces.
PARMESAN RINDS Freeze in small bags. Add to stocks (see pages 40 & 41), pasta sauces, and soups.
CELERY LEAVES Use the entire stalk including the leaves in stocks and soups; use the young leaves in salads.

ENVIRONMENTAL VEGETARIANISM

A RECENT UNITED NATIONS REPORT ANNOUNCED THAT A SWITCH TO A VEGETARIAN DIET IS PREFERABLE, SINCE A DISPROPORTIONATE AMOUNT OF GRAIN IS REQUIRED TO REAR AND FEED CATTLE THAN IF THE GRAIN ALONE WERE FOR HUMAN CONSUMPTION. EATING LESS MEAT IS A SUREFIRE WAY TO LESSEN THE IMPACT OF CLIMATE CHANGE AND WORLD HUNGER.

Make a super "fridge" soup with leftover random vegetables, any half-used cans of beans or tomatoes—finish off with rice, pasta, or quinoa. Or create Asian flavors with chopped cilantro stems and roots, lemongrass, ginger, and star anise mixed with Asian greens, broccoli, and carrot. Raid the pantry for tamari and rice or vermicelli noodles if you have them.

USE-BY & BEST-BEFORE DATES Foods with use-by dates cannot be legally sold beyond that date, while products with best-before dates can. Low-risk items such as fruits and vegetables are generally fine beyond the package date. Use common sense; look for visual clues such as mold, and smell for freshness. Arrange items in your fridge with the older items up front, dates visible, so you can easily see what needs using first.

FOOD
for thought

TO REDUCE FOOD WASTE, LOOK BEFORE YOU SHOP. CHECK YOUR FRIDGE, FREEZER AND PANTRY, THEN PLAN A MENU AROUND THE INGREDIENTS YOU ALREADY HAVE BEFORE GOING TO THE SUPERMARKET.

MONEY $AVER

1 CUP DRIED BEANS IS HALF THE PRICE OF 1 CUP CANNED

WASTE NOT
want not

FLAVOR MAKERS

SMOKED PAPRIKA & RED PEPPER FLAKES

Add this duo to beans, starchy vegetables, carbs, and proteins such as quinoa, brown rice, and tofu, for a smoky and hot taste.

CORIANDER & CUMIN SEEDS

Toast and crush these seeds, then sprinkle over Mediterranean vegetables (tomatoes, zucchini, eggplant, fennel) or carrots and zucchini. Top with spoonfuls of labne.

FENNEL SEEDS & RED PEPPER FLAKES

Sprinkle these over slices of haloumi then broil or pan-fry; or stir them through French-style green lentils with lots of chopped mint and parsley.

TURMERIC & MUSTARD SEEDS

Sauté together until the seeds pop; toss together with just-steamed green beans and toasted desiccated coconut for an earthy, slightly pungent taste.

VEG IT UP!
LEAVE THE CHICKEN OUT OF THE GUACAMOLE.

Roasted corn & QUINOA CHOWDER

PREP + COOK TIME 1 HOUR 30 MINUTES SERVES 6

Quinoa is one of only a handful of vegetarian ingredients that on their own contain all nine essential amino acids, making it a perfect meat substitute.

4 ears corn, husks and silks removed

¼ cup olive oil

4 x 8½-inch whole-grain tortillas

cooking oil spray

1 large yellow onion, chopped finely

1 large potato, chopped coarsely

2 cloves garlic, crushed

1 teaspoon red pepper flakes

¼ teaspoon smoked paprika

4 cups vegetable stock (see page 40)

½ cup cream

⅓ cup red or white quinoa

¾ cup water

⅓ cup fresh cilantro leaves

CHICKEN GUACAMOLE

⅔ cup shredded, cooked chicken breast

½ teaspoon smoked paprika

1 medium avocado, chopped coarsely

1 green onion, sliced thinly

2 tablespoons fresh cilantro leaves

2 tablespoons lime juice

1 Preheat oven to 350°F. Grease and line a baking sheet with parchment paper.

2 Place corn on baking sheet, drizzle with 1 tablespoon of the olive oil; season. Roast corn for 45 minutes, turning occasionally, or until golden and tender. Using a sharp knife, cut kernels from cobs; discard cobs.

3 Increase oven temperature to 400°F.

4 Place tortillas on two baking sheets; spray with oil. Bake for 5 minutes or until golden and crisp; break into pieces.

5 Heat remaining olive oil in a large saucepan over medium heat; cook corn kernels, onion, and potato, covered, for 10 minutes or until onion softens. Add garlic, pepper flakes, and paprika; cook, stirring, for 1 minute or until fragrant.

6 Add stock and cream; bring to a boil over high heat. Reduce heat to medium; cook, covered, for 10 minutes or until potato is tender. Remove from heat; let stand 10 minutes. Blend or process half the chowder until almost smooth; return to pan. Season to taste. Stir over heat until hot.

7 Meanwhile, place quinoa and the water in a small saucepan; bring to a boil. Reduce heat to low; cook, covered, for 12 minutes or until tender. Let stand, covered, for 10 minutes; fluff with a fork. Stir quinoa through chowder.

8 Make Chicken Guacamole.

9 Ladle chowder into bowls; top with guacamole and cilantro. Serve with tortilla chips.

chicken guacamole Combine chicken and paprika in a small bowl. Add avocado, green onion, cilantro, and juice; toss to combine. Season to taste.

tip You will need 2 limes for this recipe.

The green TURKEY BURGER

PREP + COOK TIME 45 MINUTES (+ STANDING & REFRIGERATION) MAKES 6

⅓ cup quinoa flakes

¼ cup milk

1 small zucchini, grated coarsely

1 small purple carrot, grated coarsely

2 small red onions, 1 grated coarsely + 1 thined slicely

¾ pound ground turkey or chicken

1 tablespoon finely chopped fresh flat-leaf parsley

2 tablespoons olive oil

1 small orange sweet potato, cut into ½-inch rounds

12 large iceberg lettuce leaves, cut into 4-inch rounds

1 large tomato, sliced thinly

GREEN TAHINI

¼ cup tahini

2 tablespoons fresh flat-leaf parsley leaves

2 tablespoons lemon juice

1 tablespoon olive oil

1 small clove garlic, crushed

1 Make Green Tahini.

2 Combine quinoa flakes and milk in a small bowl; let stand for 10 minutes.

3 Combine zucchini, carrot, grated onion, turkey, parsley, and quinoa mixture in a medium bowl; season to taste. Using damp hands, shape turkey mixture into six 3¼-inch patties; cover, refrigerate for 30 minutes.

4 Heat half the oil in a large non-stick frying pan over low heat; cook sweet potato, turning, for 8 minutes or until tender.

5 Heat remaining oil over medium heat; cook patties, for 4 minutes each side or until golden and cooked through.

6 Top six lettuce rounds with patties, tomato, onion slices, and sweet potato. Drizzle with Green Tahini; top with remaining lettuce rounds. Serve immediately.

green tahini Process ingredients until smooth; season to taste.

tips You will need about 1 or 2 heads of lettuce, depending on their size. Carrots were originally purple, before the 17th century and the Dutch bred an orange strain. Purple carrots boast beta-carotene and vitamin A, like their orange cousins, and additionally carry the purple-colored pigment anthocyanin, an antioxidant said to act as an anti-inflammatory.

VEG IT UP!

REPLACE TURKEY PATTIES WITH PAN-FRIED HALOUMI OR FRIED PORTOBELLO MUSHROOMS.

VEG IT UP!
INSTEAD OF CHICKEN,
USE OYSTER MUSHROOMS;
COOK THEM IN THE PAN
FOR 3 MINUTES OR
UNTIL TENDER.

Broccolini, asparagus & MISO CHICKEN SALAD

PREP + COOK TIME 25 MINUTES (+ REFRIGERATION) SERVES 4

Miso is a living fermented product that's good for gut health. It also contains naturally occurring glutamates, which gives it a very craveable taste.

2 tablespoons white miso (shiro) paste

2 tablespoons mirin

2 tablespoons olive oil

¾ pound chicken breast fillets, halved horizontally

⅓ pound broccolini, halved lengthwise

⅓ pound asparagus, trimmed, halved on the diagonal

½ cup toasted cashews, chopped coarsely

1 cup fresh cilantro leaves

1 cup fresh mint leaves

CREAMY MISO DRESSING

3 teaspoons brazil and cashew nut spread

1 tablespoon white miso (shiro) paste

1 tablespoon mirin

2 teaspoons water

1 tablespoon olive oil

¼ teaspoon sesame oil

1 Make Creamy Miso Dressing.

2 Combine miso, mirin, and half the oil in a medium bowl. Add chicken; turn to coat. Cover; refrigerate for 1 hour.

3 Boil, steam or microwave broccolini and asparagus until tender; drain. Cover to keep warm.

4 Heat remaining oil in a medium non-stick frying pan over high heat; cook chicken for 2 minutes on each side or until browned and cooked through. Cool for 5 minutes, then shred coarsely.

5 Place chicken, broccolini, and asparagus in a large bowl with cashews, herbs and dressing; toss to combine.

creamy miso dressing Place ingredients in a small screw-top jar; shake well until smooth.

tips White miso (shiro) is sweeter and milder in taste than brown, red, and black miso, making it perfect for dressings. It is available from most well-stocked supermarkets and Asian food stores. You will need 1 bunch of broccolini and 1 bunch of asparagus for this recipe.

Roasted kale &
GRILLED CHICKEN SALAD

PREP + COOK TIME 50 MINUTES SERVES 4

¾ pound green curly kale

¼ cup olive oil

¾ pound baby carrots, trimmed, halved lengthwise

¾ pound chicken breast fillets

½ small red onion, sliced thinly

½ cup small fresh flat-leaf parsley leaves

2 tablespoons pepitas (pumpkin seeds), toasted

LEMON MUSTARD DRESSING

⅓ cup mayonnaise

1 teaspoon finely grated lemon zest

2 tablespoons lemon juice

2 teaspoons dijon mustard

1 small clove garlic, crushed

1 Preheat oven to 350°F. Line three baking sheets with parchment paper.

2 Cut leaves from kale; discarding stems. Place kale on two baking sheets; drizzle with 1 tablespoon of the oil. Place carrots on remaining baking sheet; drizzle with half the remaining oil. Roast carrots for 30 minutes or until tender, adding kale to oven for the last 10 minutes of cooking time or until kale is crisp.

3 Meanwhile, cut chicken fillets in half horizontally to form four thin fillets; drizzle with remaining oil. Cook chicken on heated lightly oiled grill pan (or broil or grill) until browned and cooked through; slice thickly.

4 Make Lemon Mustard Dressing.

5 Place kale, carrot, onion, chicken, dressing, and half the parsley in a large bowl; toss to combine. Serve salad topped with remaining parsley and pepitas.

lemon mustard dressing Combine ingredients in a small bowl; season to taste.

tip You will need 1 bunch of kale.

VEG IT UP!
OMIT CHICKEN AND STEP 3. ADD TWO 400G CANS DRAINED, RINSED CHICKPEAS TO BAKING SHEET WITH THE CARROTS IN STEP 2.

VEG IT UP!
SKIP THE PROSCIUTTO
AND COOK 1 LARGE THICKLY
SLICED ZUCCHINI WITH
THE EGGPLANT.

Eggplant, prosciutto & FETA SALAD

PREP + COOK TIME 35 MINUTES SERVES 4

4 slices prosciutto (about 2 ounces)

¼ pound sourdough bread, torn into pieces

2 tablespoons olive oil

8 lebanese eggplants, cut into thirds lengthwise

½ pound mixed baby tomatoes, halved

2 tablespoons small fresh basil leaves

2 tablespoons small fresh mint leaves

2½ ounces feta, crumbled

POMEGRANATE DRESSING

1 small clove garlic, crushed

1 tablespoon pomegranate molasses

3 teaspoons sherry vinegar

¼ cup olive oil

pinch red pepper flakes

1 Preheat oven to 400°F. Line two baking sheets with parchment paper.

2 Place prosciutto on one baking sheet. Place bread on second baking sheet; drizzle bread with half the oil. Bake prosciutto and bread for 15 minutes or until both are golden and crisp.

3 Meanwhile, drizzle eggplant with remaining oil; cook eggplant on a lightly oiled grill pan (or broil or grill), for 3 minutes each side or until golden and tender.

4 Make Pomegranate Dressing.

5 Combine eggplant, tomatoes, herbs, and feta; drizzle with dressing. Serve topped with prosciutto and bread.

pomegranate dressing Combine ingredients in a small bowl; season to taste.

Chickpea, chorizo & PINE NUT STEW

PREP + COOK TIME 35 MINUTES SERVES 4

1 tablespoon olive oil

1 medium yellow onion, chopped finely

2 cloves garlic, crushed

1 fresh long red chile, chopped finely

1 can (14.5 oz) diced tomatoes

1 cup tomato sauce

1 jar (9 oz) piquillo peppers, drained, chopped coarsely

1 cup vegetable stock (see page 40) or water

¼ teaspoon saffron threads

2 cans (15 oz) chickpeas

1 cured chorizo sausage, chopped finely

1½ tablespoons toasted pine nuts

¼ cup finely grated manchego cheese (see tip)

¼ cup fresh flat-leaf parsley leaves

1 Heat oil in a large saucepan over medium-high heat; cook onion, stirring, for 5 minutes or until onion softens. Add garlic and chile; cook, stirring, for 1 minute or until fragrant.

2 Add tomatoes, tomato sauce, peppers, stock, saffron, and chickpeas; bring to a boil. Reduce heat; simmer, uncovered, for 15 minutes or until reduced slightly.

3 Meanwhile, heat a small frying pan over medium heat; cook chorizo, stirring, for 5 minutes or until golden and crisp. Drain on paper towels.

4 Serve stew topped with chorizo, pine nuts, cheese, and parsley leaves.

tip Manchego is a semi-firm Spanish sheep's milk cheese available from supermarkets, cheese shops, or delis. You can use parmesan or pecorino cheese instead.

serving suggestion Serve with sourdough bread.

VEG IT UP!
TO MAKE THIS DISH
VEGETARIAN SIMPLY
LEAVE OUT
THE CHORIZO.

VEG IT UP!
FORGET THE HAM
AND REPLACE IT WITH
4 SLICES DRAINED, SLICED,
ROASTED RED BELL PEPPER.

Caramelized onion, HAM & PECORINO STRATA

PREP + COOK TIME 1 HOUR (+ STANDING) SERVES 4

If you have any leftover stale bread, save it to use in this savory bread pudding.

2 tablespoons olive oil

2 medium yellow onions, sliced thinly

3 teaspoons finely chopped fresh rosemary

8 eggs

2 cups milk

⅔ cup finely grated pecorino cheese or parmesan

⅓ pound shaved ham, chopped coarsely

2 tablespoons smoked almonds, chopped coarsely

1 pound whole-grain sourdough bread, torn

1 pound vine-ripened cherry tomatoes

¼ cup small fresh basil leaves

1 Preheat oven to 400°F.

2 Heat half the oil in a large frying pan over medium-high heat; cook onion, stirring, for 15 minutes or until onion caramelizes. Add rosemary; cook, stirring, for 1 minute or until fragrant.

3 Whisk eggs, milk, and half the cheese in a large jug. Combine onions, ham, and almonds in a medium bowl. Layer bread and ham mixture among four 2-cup (500ml) ovenproof dishes. Pour over egg mixture; sprinkle with remaining cheese. Let stand for 20 minutes.

4 Bake for 35 minutes or until just set, golden, and puffed.

5 Meanwhile, cut tomatoes into four clusters; place on a baking sheet, drizzle with remaining oil. Roast for the last 10 minutes of strata cooking time or until skins start to split.

6 Serve strata topped with tomatoes and basil.

serving suggestion Serve with a mixed garden salad.

Chicken & POTATO STIR-FRY

PREP + COOK TIME 45 MINUTES (+ STANDING) SERVES 4

This is an unusual Sichuan Chinese recipe that features potato, an ingredient not often seen in Chinese cooking, cut into fine noodle-like strips.

2 medium potatoes, cut into fine matchsticks (see tips)

½ teaspoon flaky sea salt

1 tablespoon ground cumin

2 tablespoons rice flour

2 teaspoons red pepper flakes

½ pound chicken breast strips

1 tablespoon sesame oil

3 cloves garlic, chopped finely

¾ pound chinese water spinach, trimmed, cut into 4-inch lengths

2 tablespoons light soy sauce

¼ cup malt vinegar

½ teaspoon superfine sugar

2 fresh long green chiles, sliced thinly on the diagonal

1 Place potatoes and salt in a large bowl, cover with cold water; let stand for 15 minutes. Drain; pat dry with paper towel.

2 Meanwhile, combine cumin, flour, and half the pepper flakes in a shallow bowl. Coat chicken in spice mixture; shake away excess.

3 Heat half the oil in a wok over high heat; stir-fry chicken for 3 minutes or until just cooked through. Remove from wok.

4 Heat remaining oil in wok over medium-high heat; stir-fry garlic and potatoes for 5 minutes or until potatoes are tender. Add spinach; cook for 1 minute or until wilted.

5 Meanwhile, combine soy sauce, vinegar, sugar, and remaining pepper flakes in a small bowl; stir until sugar dissolves. Return chicken to wok with soy mixture and green chiles; stir-fry until heated through.

tips You can use any variety of waxy potatoes. For less heat, remove the seeds and the membrane from the chiles first.

serving suggestion Serve with coarsely chopped peanuts and cilantro sprigs.

VEG IT UP!
REPLACE THE CHICKEN
WITH TOFU. REPLACE
LIGHT SOY SAUCE WITH
TAMARI TO ALSO MAKE IT
GLUTEN-FREE.

VEG IT UP!
SKIP THE CHICKEN.
INCREASE THE RICE TO
¾ POUND AND
THE SPINACH TO 1¼ POUNDS.

Chicken HUNZA PIE

PREP + COOK TIME 1 HOUR 35 MINUTES (+ REFRIGERATION) SERVES 4

This green leaf and cheese pie was put on the food map by happy and healthy hippies during the '60s and '70s. Any leftovers can be reheated very well.

1½ cups all-purpose flour

1 cup whole-grain all-purpose flour

½ cup plus 1 tablespoon cold butter, chopped coarsely

4 eggs

2 tablespoons olive oil

6 cups water

⅓ pound chicken breast fillet

½ pound spinach, trimmed, chopped coarsely

2 cloves garlic, chopped finely

½ pound packaged brown microwave rice

6½ ounces feta, crumbled

2 cups ricotta

3 green onions, chopped finely

1 cup coarsely chopped fresh flat-leaf parsley

1 Process flours and butter until crumbly. Whisk together 2 eggs, 1 tablespoon of the oil, and 1 tablespoon water in a small bowl until combined. Add to flour mixture; process until mixture almost forms a dough. Knead pastry on a floured surface until smooth.

2 Roll dough between sheets of floured parchment paper into a ½-inch thick, 12¾-inch round, large enough to line a 9½-inch springform pan. Lift pastry into pan; press over base and three-quarters of the way up the side. Refrigerate 30 minutes.

3 Preheat oven to 350°F.

4 Bring the water to a boil in a large saucepan. Add chicken; return to a boil. Reduce heat; simmer, partially covered, for 12 minutes or until chicken is cooked through. Remove chicken; cool 10 minutes, then shred coarsely.

5 Return water to a boil; cook spinach for 1 minute or until wilted. Drain, rinse under cold water; drain. Squeeze out excess water.

6 Lightly beat remaining eggs in a large bowl. Add spinach, chicken, garlic, rice, feta, ricotta, green onions, and parsley; stir to combine. Fill pie crust with chicken filling.

7 Bake pie for 50 minutes or until pie is cooked through and crust is golden.

serving suggestion Serve with a green salad and lemon wedges.

Chicken pastilla TRIANGLES

PREP + COOK TIME 1 HOUR 15 MINUTES (+ STANDING) MAKES 8

Pastilla is a traditional Moroccan pie served on special occasions.

pinch saffron threads

1 tablespoon hot water

2 tablespoons olive oil, plus more for brushing

2 medium red onions, chopped finely

2 cloves garlic, crushed

1 teaspoon ground turmeric

1 teaspoon ground ginger

¾ teaspoon ground cinnamon

1 pound ground free-range chicken

1 cup toasted whole blanched almonds, chopped coarsely

1 cup coarsely chopped fresh cilantro

1 cup coarsely chopped fresh flat-leaf parsley

8 sheets filo pastry

1 Combine saffron and the water in a small bowl; set aside.

2 Heat 2 tablespoons oil in a large frying pan over medium-high heat; cook onions, garlic, turmeric, ginger, and ½ teaspoon ground cinnamon for 5 minutes or until onion softens. Add chicken; cook, stirring, for 5 minutes or until chicken browns. Season with salt. Add saffron mixture; cook for 1 minute or until water evaporates. Transfer to a large bowl. Stir in almonds, cilantro, and parsley; set aside to cool completely.

3 Preheat oven to 350°F.

4 Brush one sheet of pastry with a little oil, cut in half lengthwise, top with remaining strip. Place ½ cup chicken mixture in a corner of the pastry strip, leaving a ½-inch border. Fold opposite corner of pastry diagonally across filling to form a triangle; continue folding to end of pastry sheet, retaining triangular shape. Place on a lightly oiled baking sheet, seam-side down; repeat with remaining pastry, oil, and chicken filling.

5 Brush triangles with a little more oil; dust with remaining cinnamon. Bake for 50 minutes or until browned lightly.

serving suggestion Serve with yogurt, lemon wedges, and cilantro leaves.

VEG IT UP!
REPLACE THE CHICKEN
WITH FINELY CHOPPED
CAULIFLOWER
FLORETS.

VEG IT UP!
SKIP THE PROSCIUTTO
AND INCREASE THE
RICOTTA, PARMESAN, AND
BREAD CRUMBS.

"Meatball" & MACARONI SOUP

PREP + COOK TIME 45 MINUTES (+ REFRIGERATION) SERVES 4

The meatballs aren't true meatballs, of course—they are made of ricotta and walnuts with just a touch of prosciutto which can easily be omitted.

3 cups fresh bread crumbs

2 tablespoons plus 2 cups water

1 cup coarsely chopped toasted walnuts

1 cup ricotta

¾ cup finely grated parmesan, plus more for serving

5 slices prosciutto (about 3 ounces), chopped finely

2 eggs, beaten lightly

¼ cup finely chopped fresh basil plus 2 tablespoons small fresh basil leaves

8 cups vegetable stock (see page 40) or chicken stock

¼ pound macaroni

1 Combine bread crumbs and 2 tablespoons water in a large bowl; let stand for 5 minutes. Add nuts, ricotta, ¾ cup parmesan, prosciutto, egg, and chopped basil; season. Using damp hands, roll level tablespoons of mixture into balls; place on a baking sheet. Refrigerate 30 minutes.

2 Bring stock and 2 cups water to a boil in a large saucepan. Add ricotta balls; reduce heat, simmer, for 6 minutes. Add pasta to pan; bring to a boil. Reduce heat; simmer until pasta is tender.

3 Season soup to taste. Ladle soup into bowls; serve topped with basil leaves and parmesan.

tip You can use ground chicken instead of the prosciutto.

VEGETABLE STOCK

PREP + COOK TIME 2 HOURS 30 MINUTES
MAKES 10 CUPS

Stock is simple to prepare and will boost the flavor of any dish. The key to preparing flavorful stocks is a gentle simmer. If you boil the stock, it will not have a well-developed flavor.

Coarsely chop 1 medium leek, 1 large unpeeled yellow onion, 2 large carrots, 1 large rutabaga, 2 celery stalks (with leaves), and 3 unpeeled garlic cloves. Place vegetables in a stockpot with 1 teaspoon black peppercorns, 1 bouquet garni (see tips opposite) and 20 cups water; bring to a boil. Reduce heat; simmer, uncovered, for 2 hours. Strain stock through a sieve into a large heatproof bowl; discard solids. Allow stock to cool. Cover; refrigerate until cold.

ITALIAN-STYLE STOCK

ASIAN-STYLE STOCK

ITALIAN-STYLE STOCK

Coarsely chop 2 large unpeeled yellow onions, 2 large carrots, 2 celery stalks (with leaves) and 3 unpeeled cloves garlic. Place ingredients in a stockpot with 1 teaspoon black peppercorns, 1 bouquet garni (see tips), 1 parmesan rind, 1 teaspoon fennel seeds, 12½ ounces canned whole peeled tomatoes, and 20 cups water. Cook following the directions for vegetable stock (opposite page).

ASIAN-STYLE STOCK

Coarsely chop 1 medium leek, 2 large carrots, 2 celery stalks (with leaves), 3 unpeeled cloves garlic, 4-inch piece fresh ginger, and 4 green onions. Place ingredients in a stockpot with 1 teaspoon black peppercorns, 20 sprigs fresh cilantro, 1 cinnamon stick, 3 whole star anise, ½ cup tamari, and 20 cups water. Cook following the directions for vegetable stock (opposite page).

TIPS

To make a bouquet garni, tie 3 fresh bay leaves, 2 sprigs fresh rosemary, 6 sprigs fresh thyme, and 6 fresh flat-leaf parsley stalks together with kitchen string.

Keep vegetable peelings from your meal preparations in a bowl in the fridge and add them to your stock. This is very sustainable and adds great flavor.

Prepare your stock a day ahead and leave overnight before you strain it. This will allow the flavors to infuse and create a stronger tasting stock. Freeze any leftover stock in ice cube trays for later use.

VEG IT UP!
USE SOY SAUCE OR SALT
INSTEAD OF FISH SAUCE
AND REPLACE CHICKEN
WITH MIXED
MUSHROOMS.

Chicken & noodles in
SPICED COCONUT WATER

PREP + COOK TIME 35 MINUTES   SERVES 4

4 cups coconut water (see tip)

1 tablespoon finely grated ginger

2 cloves garlic, chopped finely

¼ cup fish sauce

1 ounce palm sugar, grated coarsely

½ pound chicken breast fillets

1¼ pounds cooked rice noodles

2 persian cucumbers, halved lengthwise, sliced thinly on the diagonal

4 green onions, sliced thinly

2 cups bean sprouts

¾ cup fresh cilantro leaves

¾ cup fresh mint leaves

½ cup fresh thai basil leaves

1 fresh long red chile, sliced thinly on the diagonal

⅓ cup toasted slivered almonds

1 medium lime, cut into wedges

1 Bring coconut water, ginger, garlic, fish sauce, and sugar to a boil in a large saucepan. Add chicken; return to a boil. Reduce heat; simmer, covered, for 12 minutes or until chicken is cooked through. Remove chicken; cool 10 minutes. Shred chicken coarsely.

2 Return broth mixture to a boil. Reduce heat; simmer, uncovered, for 10 minutes or until broth has reduced slightly. Remove from heat.

3 Add chicken and noodles to broth; let stand for 5 minutes or until warmed through. Divide mixture among bowls; top with cucumber, onion, sprouts, herbs, chile, and almonds. Serve with lime wedges.

tip Make sure you buy pure coconut water that hasn't been sweetened.

Peach caprese salad
WITH CHICKEN SKEWERS

PREP + COOK TIME 25 MINUTES SERVES 4

¾ pound chicken breast fillets, cubed

1½ tablespoons chile oil

4 medium peaches, sliced thickly

1 ball buffalo mozzarella, torn

4 medium heirloom tomatoes, sliced thinly

½ cup fresh small basil leaves

1 tablespoon white wine vinegar

PISTACHIO MINT PESTO

½ cup pistachios

1½ cups fresh mint leaves

1 cup fresh flat-leaf parsley leaves

1 clove garlic, crushed

2 teaspoons finely grated lemon zest

2 teaspoons lemon juice

½ cup extra-virgin olive oil

1 Make Pistachio Mint Pesto.

2 Combine chicken and 1 tablespoon of the oil in a medium bowl; season. Thread onto four skewers.

3 Cook chicken on a lightly oiled heated griddle (or under a broiler or on a grill) for 10 minutes, adding peaches for the last 2 minutes of chicken cooking time or until chicken is cooked through and peaches are golden.

4 On a platter, layer peaches with mozzarella, tomatoes, and basil; drizzle with vinegar and remaining oil. Serve salad with chicken and pesto.

pistachio mint pesto Blend or process ingredients until smooth; season to taste.

tips Buffalo mozzarella has a tangier flavor than cow's milk mozzarella, which may be substituted. If you use bamboo skewers, quickly soak them first by placing them in a tall jug; fill with boiling water and let stand for 5 minutes.

VEG IT UP!
REPLACE CHICKEN SKEWERS WITH GRILLED ASPARAGUS, TOFU, OR EGGPLANT.

VEG IT UP!
SKIP THE BACON AND
USE FIRM FETA CHUNKS
OR CORN KERNELS
INSTEAD.

Smoky tomato & BACON FRITTERS

PREP + COOK TIME 40 MINUTES (+ STANDING) SERVES 4

Avocados offer a rich supply of 14 different minerals and vitamins, as well as heart-friendly monosaturated fatty acids.

½ pound thick bacon slices, chopped coarsely

3 cloves garlic, crushed

¾ pound ripe tomatoes, chopped finely

2 teaspoons smoked paprika

2 tablespoons chopped fresh chives

2 eggs

⅓ cup milk

1 cup spelt flour

½ teaspoon baking powder

1 medium avocado

½ cup mayonnaise

1 tablespoon lemon juice

2 tablespoons olive oil

1 large fennel bulb, sliced thinly

2 tablespoons chopped fresh chives

1 Heat a large, non-stick frying pan over high heat; cook bacon until golden and crisp. Transfer to a large bowl.

2 Add 2 cloves garlic, tomato, paprika, 1 tablespoon chives, eggs, and milk; stir to combine. Add combined sifted flour and baking powder; season and stir to combine. Let stand for 15 minutes.

3 Meanwhile, blend or process avocado flesh, mayonnaise, juice, and remaining garlic until smooth. Season to taste.

4 Heat oil in same frying pan over medium heat. Spoon 2 tablespoonfuls of batter into pan; cook for 2 minutes or until bubbles appear. Turn fritters; cook until other side is lightly browned. Repeat with remaining mixture to make 8 fritters in total.

5 Combine fennel and remaining chives in a small bowl.

6 Serve fritters with fennel salad and avocado mixture.

Sweet potato, prosciutto & SMOKED MOZZARELLA FLATBREADS

PREP + COOK TIME 45 MINUTES SERVES 4

¾ pound sweet potato, sliced thinly

8 flatbread wraps or lavash

1 cup finely grated parmesan

8 slices prosciutto (about ¼ pound), torn

¼ cup fresh sage leaves

2 teaspoons finely grated lemon zest

½ pound smoked mozzarella, sliced thinly

2½ ounces baby arugula leaves

1½ tablespoons balsamic vinegar

1 tablespoon olive oil

4 large fresh figs, quartered

1 Preheat oven to 425°F. Line four baking sheets with parchment paper.

2 Cook sweet potatoes in boiling water for 5 minutes or until tender; drain.

3 Place four wraps on baking sheets; sprinkle with parmesan. Top with remaining wraps, then sweet potato, prosciutto, sage, zest, and mozzarella. Bake, in two batches, for 12 minutes or until golden and crisp.

4 Combine arugula, vinegar, and oil in a large bowl. Divide figs and arugula mixture between flatbreads.

VEG IT UP!
SKIP THE PROSCIUTTO
AND INCREASE
THE AMOUNT OF SWEET
POTATOES TO 1 POUND.

VEG IT UP!
SKIP THE PORK
AND USE GRILLED
HALOUMI SLICES
INSTEAD.

Beet, blood orange & PORK SALAD

PREP + COOK TIME 40 MINUTES SERVES 4

½ pound pork fillet, trimmed

1 whole-grain baguette, halved horizontally, halved crosswise

2 tablespoons olive oil

1 can (14 oz) baby beets, halved

3 small blood oranges, peeled, sliced thinly

3 ounces radicchio leaves, torn

2½ ounces mesclun salad leaves

8 fresh pitted dates, halved

½ cup pitted kalamata olives, halved

2 tablespoons pepitas (pumpkin seeds), toasted

2 tablespoons sunflower seeds, toasted

2 teaspoons poppy seeds

RASPBERRY ORANGE BLOSSOM DRESSING

2 tablespoons raspberry wine vinegar

2 tablespoons olive oil

1 tablespoon orange blossom water

1 small clove garlic, crushed

2 teaspoons chopped fresh chives

1 Make Raspberry Orange Blossom Dressing.
2 Drizzle pork and bread with oil; season. Cook pork on a lightly oiled heated grill pan (or on a grill or under a broiler), turning frequently, for 15 minutes or until cooked through. Rest for 5 minutes before slicing thickly. Place bread on the oiled heated grill pan for 2 minutes each side or until golden. Tear bread into large pieces.
3 Place pork in a large bowl with beets, blood oranges, radicchio, mesclun, dates, olives, and dressing; toss to combine. Sprinkle salad with seeds, serve with bread.
raspberry orange blossom dressing Combine ingredients in a small bowl; season to taste.

tip You can use grilled chicken breast or thigh fillets instead of the pork, if you like.

Lemon thyme chicken
WITH CAPERBERRY SALSA

PREP + COOK TIME 50 MINUTES (+ STANDING) SERVES 4

4 chicken breast supreme (see tips)

¼ cup olive oil

2 tablespoons fresh thyme leaves, plus sprigs for garnish

1 tablespoon finely grated lemon zest

1 celery root, peeled

2 large carrots

1 clove garlic, crushed

2 tablespoons white balsamic vinegar

½ cup toasted pepitas (pumpkin seeds)

¾ cup coarsely chopped fresh flat-leaf parsley, plus leaves for garnish

2 tablespoons Greek-style yogurt

CAPERBERRY SALSA

1 cup caperberries

2 tablespoons olive oil

2 tablespoons lemon juice

1½ teaspoons dried pink peppercorns, crushed coarsely

1 Preheat oven to 425°F. Line a baking sheet with parchment paper.

2 Combine chicken, 1 tablespoon oil, thyme leaves, and zest in a large bowl; let stand for 10 minutes.

3 Meanwhile, using a vegetable peeler, peel long thin ribbons from the celery root and carrots (keep the center core of each vegetable for another use, see tips). Place vegetable ribbons in a large bowl with garlic, vinegar, pepitas, chopped parsley, and yogurt; season. Stir to combine.

4 Heat a large frying pan over medium-high heat; cook chicken for 3 minutes each side or until browned all over. Transfer to baking sheet; roast for 12 minutes or until cooked through.

5 Meanwhile, make Caperberry Salsa.

6 Serve chicken with vegetable salad and salsa; garnish with thyme sprigs and parsley leaves.

caperberry salsa Halve three-quarters of the caperberries, keeping the stems attached; reserve remaining for serving. Combine halved caperberries in a small bowl with oil, juice, and peppercorns.

tips Chicken breast supreme is a chicken breast with the skin and wing bone attached. Ask your butcher to prepare it for you or use skinless chicken breast fillets instead. You can use the remaining center core of the celery root and carrot in a soup.

VEG IT UP!
REPLACE THE CHICKEN
WITH PAN-FRIED
HALOUMI SLICES.

Everyday
VEGE-QUARIAN

*For the lacto-ovo vegetarian who is happy
to eat fish and seafood (aka pescetarian).
These recipes contain no meat.*

Snapper ceviche tacos
WITH PICKLED RADISH

PREP + COOK TIME 45 MINUTES **(+ STANDING) SERVES** 4

2 cups shredded white cabbage

½ cup coarsely chopped fresh cilantro

¼ cup lime juice

¼ cup olive oil

1 cup sour cream

1 tablespoon sriracha or other hot chile sauce

¾ pound snapper or halibut, cut into ½-inch pieces

2 green onions, sliced thinly

8 x 2¾-inch white corn tortillas

2 medium avocados, chopped coarsely

2 tablespoons fresh oregano leaves

PICKLED RADISH

1 teaspoon cumin seeds

¼ cup apple cider vinegar

1 teaspoon superfine sugar

pinch sea salt flakes

6 radishes, trimmed, sliced thinly

1 Make Pickled Radish.

2 Meanwhile, combine cabbage, cilantro, 1 tablespoon of the juice, and 1 tablespoon of the oil in a medium bowl; season to taste.

3 Combine sour cream and hot sauce in a small bowl; season to taste.

4 Combine fish, green onions, remaining juice, and 1 tablespoon of the oil in a large glass or ceramic bowl. Cover; refrigerate for 25 minutes or until fish is opaque and cured.

5 Meanwhile, cook tortillas on a lightly oiled heated grill pan (or under the broiler) for 30 seconds each side or until golden and warmed through.

6 Serve tortillas topped with cabbage salad, fish, avocado, pickled radish, sour cream mixture, and oregano; drizzle with remaining oil.

pickled radish Stir cumin seeds in a dry frying pan over medium heat for 2 minutes or until toasted and fragrant. Place seeds in a medium bowl with vinegar, sugar, and salt; stir until sugar dissolves. Add radish; let stand for 10 minutes.

tips Ceviche is a popular South American seafood dish that 'cooks' by marinating in citrus juice. Sriracha is a medium-hot chile sauce available from well-stocked supermarkets.

Roasted trout, fennel & BUCKWHEAT SALAD

PREP + COOK TIME 1 HOUR 15 MINUTES SERVES 4

3 baby fennel, trimmed, fronds reserved

¼ cup lemon juice

¼ cup olive oil

1 small clove garlic, chopped finely

1 tablespoon finely grated lemon zest

3 skinless ocean trout fillets

1 cup buckwheat

1 cup fresh flat-leaf parsley leaves, torn

CILANTRO LEMON DRESSING

2 teaspoons coriander seeds

½ cup fresh cilantro leaves

⅓ cup lemon juice

2 tablespoons extra-virgin olive oil

1 small clove garlic, chopped finely

½ teaspoon smoked paprika

1 Preheat oven to 350°F. Line two baking sheets with parchment paper.

2 Cut two fennel bulbs into thin wedges; place on baking sheet. Thinly slice remaining fennel. Combine sliced fennel and 1 tablespoon of the juice in a small bowl; set aside.

3 Whisk oil, garlic, zest and remaining juice in a small bowl; season to taste. Drizzle half the lemon mixture over fennel wedges; roast for 35 minutes or until tender.

4 Meanwhile, place trout on second baking sheet; drizzle with remaining lemon mixture. Roast for 12 minutes or until almost cooked through; flake coarsely.

5 Heat a medium frying pan over medium heat; toast buckwheat, stirring, until light golden.

6 Cook buckwheat in a medium saucepan of boiling water for 20 minutes or until tender; drain. Cool slightly.

7 Meanwhile, make Cilantro Lemon Dressing.

8 Place roasted fennel, sliced fennel, reserved fennel fronds, trout, buckwheat, parsley, and dressing in a large bowl; toss to combine. Season to taste.

cilantro lemon dressing Place coriander seeds in a small frying pan, stir over medium heat for 2 minutes or until fragrant and toasted; cool. Grind seeds coarsely with a pestle and mortar. Process ground coriander seeds with remaining ingredients until smooth and combined. Season to taste.

Shrimp & red curry FRITTERS

PREP + COOK TIME 35 MINUTES (+ REFRIGERATION) SERVES 4

¾ pound peeled uncooked large shrimp, chopped coarsely

4 fresh kaffir lime leaves, shredded finely

1 egg

3 teaspoons thai red curry paste

1 teaspoon fish sauce

½ teaspoon grated palm sugar

¼ cup thinly sliced green beans

⅓ cup coarsely grated fresh coconut (see tips)

2½ cups shredded green papaya (see tips)

1 persian cucumber, cut into matchsticks (see tips)

½ small red onion, sliced thinly

1 cup fresh cilantro leaves

1 cup fresh thai basil leaves

½ cup toasted peanuts

2 tablespoons vegetable oil

LIME DRESSING

2 tablespoons lime juice

1 tablespoon fish sauce

1 tablespoon water

2½ teaspoons grated palm sugar

1 Process ¼ pound of the chopped shrimp with half the shredded lime leaves, egg, paste, sauce, and sugar until just smooth; transfer to a large bowl. Add beans, remaining chopped shrimp, and half the coconut; mix to combine. Season. Shape shrimp mixture into 8 fritters. Cover; refrigerate for 30 minutes.

2 Meanwhile, make Lime Dressing.

3 Place papaya, cucumber, onion, cilantro, basil, peanuts, remaining coconut, and remaining lime leaves in a large bowl with dressing; toss to combine.

4 Heat oil in a large frying pan over medium-high heat; cook fritters for 2½ minutes each side or until golden and cooked through. Serve fritters with papaya salad.

lime dressing Stir ingredients in a small bowl until sugar dissolves.

tips To open a fresh coconut, pierce one of the eyes at the top of the coconut; drain the coconut water, then roast the coconut in a 425°F oven for 15 minutes until cracks appear in the shell. Cool the coconut, then break it apart and grate the flesh. An easy way to shred the papaya and cucumber into long thin strips is to use a vegetable peeler.

VEG IT UP!
REPLACE THE SQUID
WITH EGGPLANTS.

Fattoush & BARBECUED SQUID SALAD

PREP + COOK TIME 50 MINUTES (+ REFRIGERATION) SERVES 4

1½ teaspoons cumin seeds

1 teaspoon ground coriander

2 cloves garlic, crushed

½ teaspoon red pepper flakes

¼ cup olive oil

2 tablespoons lemon juice

6 medium squid hoods (about 1½ pounds), cleaned, and tentacles

3 medium tomatoes, chopped coarsely

1½ teaspoons flaky sea salt

1 persian cucumber, halved lengthwise, seeded, chopped coarsely

1 cup fresh mint leaves

1 cup fresh flat-leaf parsley leaves

cooking oil spray

2 whole-grain pita breads, split in half

1 Stir seeds and ground coriander in a small frying pan over medium heat for 2 minutes or until toasted and fragrant. Transfer mixture to a medium bowl with garlic, pepper flakes, olive oil, and juice; stir to combine. Reserve 2 tablespoons of the spice mixture in a small bowl.

2 Place a cook's knife flat inside one of the squid hoods. Using a second knife, slice squid crosswise at ¾-inch intervals (as if you're cutting it into rings; the knife will prevent you cutting all the way through the squid). Repeat with remaining squid. Add squid hoods and tentacles to spice mixture in bowl; toss to coat. Refrigerate for 2 hours.

3 Meanwhile, place tomatoes in a colander, sprinkle with salt; let stand 10 minutes. Place tomatoes, cucumber, mint, and parsley in a medium bowl; toss to combine.

4 Cook pita and squid hoods and tentacles on a heated lightly oiled grill pan (or on a grill or under the broiler) until pita is toasted and squid is just cooked through.

5 Break pita into small pieces. Add reserved spice mixture and half the pita to tomato mixture; toss to combine. Serve squid with salad and remaining pita.

tips Use mixed heirloom tomatoes for the best taste and great color. If you are having difficulty splitting the pita breads open, microwave on high (100%) for 10 seconds. The steam from heating in the microwave usually makes it easier to open the bread.

Beer-battered fish with
JALAPEÑO & WATERMELON SALAD

PREP + COOK TIME 50 MINUTES **SERVES** 4

1¼ cups self-rising flour

⅔ cup chilled beer

2 teaspoons garlic salt

vegetable oil, for deep-frying

¾ pound firm white fish fillets, cut into thick strips

2 pita breads

JALAPEÑO & WATERMELON SALAD

2 fresh jalapeño chiles, sliced thinly

1 small red onion, sliced thinly

1 clove garlic, sliced thinly

2 tablespoons white wine vinegar

1 tablespoon superfine sugar

1 pound seedless watermelon, chopped coarsely

1 baby romaine lettuce, trimmed, leaves separated

2 small avocados, sliced thinly

1 cup fresh cilantro leaves

2 tablespoons lime juice

1 tablespoon olive oil

1 Whisk ¾ cup of the flour, the beer, and garlic salt in a medium bowl to form a thick batter; refrigerate 15 minutes.

2 Meanwhile, make Jalapeño and Watermelon Salad.

3 Fill a wok one-third with oil and heat to 350°F (or until a cube of bread browns in 15 seconds). Place remaining flour in a medium bowl. Coat fish in flour; shake away excess. Dip fish in batter; drain off excess. Deep-fry fish, in batches, until golden and cooked through. Drain on paper towels.

4 Serve fish immediately with salad and pita bread.

jalapeño & watermelon salad Combine jalapeños, onion, garlic, vinegar, and sugar in a large bowl; let stand 10 minutes. Strain jalapeño mixture; discard liquid. Return jalapeño mixture to bowl. Add watermelon, lettuce, avocado, cilantro, juice, and oil; toss to combine.

tip Snapper was used in this recipe, but you could use any firm white fish you prefer.

VEG IT UP!
REPLACE THE FISH
WITH PAN-FRIED
HALOUMI SLICES.

Pea, tarragon, shrimp & ALMOND CAKES

PREP + COOK TIME 45 MINUTES (+ REFRIGERATION) SERVES 4

1½ cups frozen peas

1 clove garlic, peeled

¼ pound peeled uncooked medium shrimp, chopped coarsely

1 tablespoon fresh tarragon leaves, chopped coarsely, plus 1 tablespoon fresh tarragon leaves

½ teaspoon finely grated lemon zest

1 tablespoon ground almonds

2 cups firmly packed trimmed watercress

1 medium fennel bulb, sliced thinly

1 stalk celery, trimmed, sliced thinly on the diagonal

¼ cup toasted whole blanched almonds, chopped coarsely

2 tablespoons olive oil

MUSTARD & LEMON DRESSING

1½ tablespoons dijon mustard

1 tablespoon lemon juice

1 tablespoon olive oil

1 Boil, steam, or microwave peas and garlic together until peas are tender; drain.

2 Blend or process garlic and 1 cup of the peas with shrimp, chopped tarragon, zest, and ground almonds until combined; season. Using oiled hands, roll level tablespoons of shrimp mixture into 16 balls; flatten slightly. Cover; refrigerate for 1 hour. (The patties are quite sticky, however they will not fall apart during cooking.)

3 Meanwhile, make Mustard and Lemon Dressing.

4 Place watercress, fennel, celery, blanched almonds, tarragon leaves, and remaining peas in a large bowl with half the dressing; toss to combine.

5 Heat oil in a large non-stick frying pan over medium heat; cook patties, in batches, for 2 minutes each side or until golden and cooked through. Cover to keep warm.

6 Serve patties with salad, drizzled with remaining dressing.

mustard & lemon dressing Whisk ingredients in a small bowl until combined; season to taste.

tips Patties can be made up to 1 day ahead; store in an airtight container in the fridge. Use a mandoline or V-slicer to slice the fennel very thinly.

Tuna salad
SUSHI BOWL

PREP + COOK TIME 35 MINUTES SERVES 4

⅓ cup teriyaki sauce

⅓ cup rice vinegar

1 tablespoon finely grated fresh ginger

¾ pound packaged brown microwave rice

2 cans (6 oz each) canned tuna in springwater, drained

1 persian cucumber, halved lengthwise, seeded, sliced thinly lengthwise

1 large avocado, sliced thinly

1 large carrot, cut into matchsticks

⅓ cup drained pickled ginger, sliced thinly

1 tablespoon sesame seeds, toasted

½ sheet toasted seaweed (nori), shredded finely

1 Combine sauce, vinegar, and ginger in a small bowl.

2 Heat rice following package instructions.

3 Combine warm rice and half the dressing in a bowl.

4 Serve rice with tuna, cucumber, avocado, carrot, and pickled ginger. Drizzle with remaining dressing; sprinkle with sesame seeds and seaweed.

Save bones for stock Ask the fishmonger to fillet whole fish for you and ask to keep the bones for stock. When you get home, fry an onion and carrot, add the bones and a little dry white wine, stirring until the bones turn opaque. Add enough water to cover and cook at a gentle simmer for 30 minutes; strain. Cool, then refrigerate. Use in 3 days or freeze for up to 1 month.

Herbs FOR Fish

SOFT LEAF HERBS Are nicest in their fresh form though you can add the sprigs and stalks to the fish cavity for extra flavor.

HERB SALAD Toss the torn leaves of cilantro, mint (any variety such as round or spearmint) and flat-leaf parsley, with thinly sliced shallots.

HARDY HERBS Rosemary and sage are too pungent to go with fish. However, thyme and bay leaves work well with oily fish.

Tangy things THAT GO WELL WITH FISH

A SQUEEZE OF LEMON OR A DASH OF VINEGAR; CORNICHONS, OR CAPERS; A DOLLOP OF DIJON MUSTARD, PLAIN YOGURT, OR CRÈME FRAÎCHE.

CHOOSE FISH WISELY

THERE ARE MANY BENEFITS TO INCLUDING SOME FISH IN YOUR DIET. WITH FISH STOCKS DEPLETED WE NEED TO MAKE SUSTAINABLE CHOICES. BUY SMALLER FISH, RATHER THAN LARGE GAME FISH (SUCH AS YELLOW FIN TUNA AND SWORDFISH, TYPES THAT ARE MOST ENDANGERED) AND TRY UNDERUTILIZED SPECIES.

YESTERDAY'S FISH MEAL ANOTHER WAY

Flake fish through steamed barley with lots of fresh herbs and cucumber.

Combine fish, quinoa, and plenty of herbs with a little egg and form into cakes; pan-fry in oil.

Add to an omelet with torn kale and capers.

Zesty Goodness If a recipe only calls for the juice of a citrus fruit, don't waste the rind. Grate it first, then measure into ½ teaspoon quantities and freeze for later use. As well as its potent citrus flavor, the rind contains two antioxidants – limonene and coumarin – which have been shown to stimulate the detoxification enzyme that helps the body get rid of potentially carcinogenic compounds.

Storing FISH

FISH IS HIGHLY PERISHABLE SO TRY TO BUY IT ON THE DAY YOU PLAN TO COOK IT. YOU CAN STORE RAW FISH AND SHRIMP, AND COOKED FISH DISHES, FOR UP TO 2 DAYS IN THE FRIDGE. MAKE SURE THAT COOKED DISHES ARE REFRIGERATED QUICKLY AND NOT LEFT TO SIT AT ROOM TEMPERATURE FOR LONG.

MONEY $AVER

USE UNDERUTILIZED FISH SPECIES AND ALSO HELP THE ENVIRONMENT.

WASTE NOT want not

HOW TO...

CRISP FISH SKIN

Pat skin dry with paper towel; sprinkle with salt. Add a little oil to a hot heavy-bottomed frying pan. Cook fish, skin-side down, pressing on it with a spatula, until crisp. Turn, cook other side.

REMOVE PIN-BONES

These small bones run adjacent to the spine of the fish, along the thickest part of the flesh. Run your fingers over the flesh to find the bones; place a finger either side of the bone then pull it out with clean tweezers.

REMOVE THE SKIN

Insert a sharp, flexible knife horizontally between the skin and the flesh; grip the skin with your other hand. Holding the knife flat, wiggle it along the fillet to detach the skin from the flesh.

COOK FISH PERFECTLY

Fish cooks quickly, and continues to cook even after it's removed from the heat. To avoid fish overcooking, take it out of the pan just before you think it's cooked. By the time it hits the plate, it should be just right.

Ginger-chile shrimp
QUINOA "FRIED RICE"

PREP + COOK TIME 35 MINUTES **(+ REFRIGERATION)** **SERVES** 4

You will need to start this recipe the day before (see tip).

1 cup quinoa

2 teaspoons peanut oil

2 teaspoons sesame oil

2 pounds uncooked medium shrimp, peeled, deveined, tails intact

2 cloves garlic, sliced thinly

¾-ounce piece fresh ginger, cut into matchsticks

1 fresh long red chile, sliced thinly

4 green onions, sliced thinly

¾ cup frozen baby peas

2 tablespoons sweet soy sauce

½ cup fresh cilantro leaves

1 Cook quinoa in a large saucepan of boiling water for 12 minutes or until tender; drain. Spread quinoa on an oven tray. Refrigerate, uncovered, overnight.
2 Heat oils in a wok over high heat; stir-fry shrimp for 1 minute or until almost cooked through. Add garlic, ginger, and half the chile; stir-fry for 1 minute or until fragrant. Add green onions and peas; stir-fry for 1 minute or until heated through.
3 Add quinoa and sweet soy sauce; stir-fry for 1 minute or until heated through. Serve topped with cilantro and remaining chile.

tip If you are short on time, cook quinoa on the day of serving, spread it over a tray and place in the freezer for 15 minutes, then continue with the recipe.

Fish banh mi with pickled vegetables & SPICY MAYONNAISE

PREP + COOK TIME 35 MINUTES
(+ REFRIGERATION) MAKES 4

2 teaspoons peanut oil

2 teaspoons sesame oil

8 small flathead fillets (about 2 pounds)

2 demi baguettes , ends trimmed, halved crosswise

1 persian cucumber, halved lengthwise, seeded, sliced thinly

1 green onion, sliced thinly on the diagonal

1 fresh long red chile, sliced thinly

8 large fresh cilantro sprigs

PICKLED VEGETABLES

½ cup granulated sugar

½ cup rice vinegar

½ teaspoon kosher salt

1 medium carrot, cut into matchsticks

¼ medium daikon radish, cut into matchsticks

SPICY MAYONNAISE

¼ cup mayonnaise

3 teaspoons sriracha or other chile sauce

1 Make Pickled Vegetables and Spicy Mayonnaise.

2 Heat oils in a large frying pan over high heat; cook fish for 2½ minutes each side or until just cooked through.

3 Split baguettes in half horizontally. Spread mayonnaise over bases; top with fish, cucumber, green onion, pickled vegetables, chile, and cilantro.

pickled vegetables Stir sugar, vinegar, and salt in a small saucepan over low heat for 2 minutes or until sugar dissolves; bring to a boil. Transfer mixture to a medium bowl; stir in carrot and daikon. Refrigerate for 1 hour. Drain.

spicy mayonnaise Combine ingredients in a small bowl; season to taste. Refrigerate until required.

tip Sriracha is a medium-hot chile sauce available from Asian food stores and well-stocked supermarkets.

Shrimp barley risotto
WITH CHILE GREMOLATA

PREP + COOK TIME 50 MINUTES   SERVES 4

1 tablespoon olive oil

1 medium yellow onion, chopped finely

2 cloves garlic, crushed

1½ cups pearl barley

4 cups vegetable stock (see page 40) or water

1 pound peeled uncooked medium shrimp

¼ cup finely grated parmesan

1½ ounces baby arugula

5 ounces labne (see tips)

CHILE GREMOLATA

1 tablespoon finely grated lemon zest (see tips)

1 fresh long red chile, seeded, chopped finely

2 tablespoons finely chopped fresh flat-leaf parsley

1 Heat oil in a large saucepan over medium-high heat; cook onion and garlic, stirring, for 5 minutes or until onion softens. Add barley; cook, stirring, for 1 minute or until coated. Add stock; bring to a boil. Reduce heat to low; simmer, covered, for 30 minutes or until barley is almost tender.

2 Add shrimp; simmer, uncovered, for 5 minutes or until barley is tender and liquid is absorbed. Add parmesan and arugula; stir to combine.

3 Make Chile Gremolata.

4 Serve risotto topped with labne and chile gremolata.

chile gremolata Combine ingredients in a small bowl.

tips Labne is a soft fresh cheese made from strained yogurt, generally it is rolled into balls and stored in olive oil. If you have one, use a zester to create strips of lemon peel instead of grating it. If you don't have one, peel two long, wide strips of rind from the lemon, without the white pith, then cut them lengthwise into thin strips.

Spinach, white bean & SHRIMP AGNOLOTTI

PREP + COOK TIME 30 MINUTES SERVES 4

1 tablespoon olive oil

3 ounces baby spinach leaves

1 clove garlic, crushed

1 can (15 oz) cannellini beans, drained, rinsed

¼ pound peeled uncooked medium shrimp, cut into ½-inch pieces

¼ cup fresh chives, chopped finely

32 round wonton wrappers

1½ cups dry white wine

1½ cups fish stock

pinch saffron threads

⅓ cup (80ml) heavy cream

1 Heat oil in a frying pan over medium-high heat; cook spinach and garlic, stirring, until spinach wilts. Drain; squeeze out excess water.

2 Roughly mash beans with the back of a fork in a large bowl. Add spinach, shrimp, and half the chives; mix to combine. Season.

3 Place 2 teaspoons of shrimp mixture in the center of one wrapper; brush around edges with water. Fold wrapper over filling; press edges together to seal. Place, in a single layer, on a baking sheet. Repeat with remaining wrappers and shrimp mixture.

4 Bring wine, stock, and saffron to a boil in a large frying pan over high heat. Reduce heat; simmer, uncovered, for 5 minutes or until reduced slightly. Stir in cream; keep warm.

5 Meanwhile, cook pasta, in batches, in a large saucepan of boiling water, for 1½ minutes or until filling is cooked through; drain.

6 Add pasta to cream mixture with remaining chives; toss to combine.

VEG IT UP!
USE CHOPPED SAUTÉED CREMINI MUSHROOMS INSTEAD OF SHRIMP AND VEGETABLE STOCK INSTEAD OF FISH STOCK.

Mussels in chile broth
WITH FREEKEH

PREP + COOK TIME 1 HOUR 35 MINUTES SERVES 4

1 cup dry white wine

2 pounds black mussels, cleaned (see tips)

1 tablespoon olive oil

1 medium yellow onion, chopped finely

2 stalks celery, trimmed, cut into ½-inch pieces

¾ pound baby carrots, sliced thinly on the diagonal

2 tablespoons tomato paste

1 cup wheat freekeh, rinsed (see tips)

½ teaspoon red pepper flakes

3 cups fish stock

1 medium lemon, cut into wedges

2 tablespoons coarsely chopped fresh flat-leaf parsley

1 Bring wine to a boil in a large saucepan over medium-high heat. Add mussels; cook, covered, for 8 minutes or until mussels open. Strain mussels through a colander into a large heatproof bowl; reserve cooking liquid. Cover mussels; set aside until required.

2 Heat oil in same saucepan over medium heat; cook onion, celery, and carrots for 3 minutes or until onion softens. Add paste, freekeh, and pepper flakes; cook, stirring, for 1 minute or until fragrant. Add stock and reserved cooking liquid; bring to a boil. Reduce heat; simmer, partially covered, for 1 hour until freekeh is tender.

3 Add mussels to pan; cook, uncovered, for 2 minutes or until heated through. Serve mussels with lemon wedges and topped with parsley.

tips If you prefer, you can buy 2-pound packs of pot-ready mussels from fishmongers or seafood markets. These are already scrubbed and bearded, and ready to cook. Some mussels might not open after cooking. These might need prompting with a knife or might not have cooked as quickly as the others – some will not open after excessive cooking. You do not have to discard these, just open with a knife and cook a little more if you like. You can use clams instead of the mussels. Freekeh is an ancient grain food made from roasted young green wheat. Nutritionally freekeh stacks up impressively; it has a low GI, four times the fiber of brown rice, is higher in protein than regular wheat, and is a good source of iron, magnesium, thiamin, copper, and zinc. Freekeh does contain gluten so is not suitable for those on gluten-free diets. Freekeh is available at health food shops and well-stocked grocery stores.

Black pepper
TOFU & SHRIMP

PREP + COOK TIME 35 MINUTES **(+ STANDING) SERVES** 4

This dish uses the flavors traditionally used to make Singaporean chile crab.

9 ounces firm tofu, cut into 1¼-inch pieces

2 tablespoons coconut oil

12 uncooked medium shrimp (about 1 pound), peeled, deveined, tails intact

⅓ pound green beans, cut into 2-inch lengths

2 tablespoons drained fermented black beans, rinsed, chopped coarsely

1½ teaspoons black peppercorns, ground coarsely (see tip)

2 cloves garlic, sliced thinly

¾-ounce piece fresh ginger, cut into matchsticks

2 tablespoons oyster sauce

1 teaspoon superfine sugar

2 tablespoons water

3 green onions, sliced thinly

1 fresh small red (serrano) chile, sliced thinly

1 Place tofu in between paper towels; let stand for 30 minutes.

2 Heat oil in a wok over high heat; stir-fry shrimp and beans for 2 minutes or until shrimp are almost cooked through. Add black beans, pepper, garlic, ginger, sauce, sugar, and the water; stir-fry for 1 minute or until combined. Add tofu and green onions; stir-fry for 1 minute or until heated through.

3 Serve immediately topped with chile slices.

tip To grind pepper coarsely, loosen the tension on your pepper mill to produce a coarser grind or alternatively use a mortar and pestle.

serving suggestion Serve with steamed jasmine rice or warmed roti.

VEG IT UP!
REPLACE SHRIMP WITH ASPARAGUS AND ASSORTED MUSHROOMS; USE A MUSHROOM-BASED VEGETARIAN OYSTER SAUCE.

Finding a good-quality vegan mayonnaise is difficult and most are soy based. This recipe is not only dairy-free and egg-free, but soy-free as well.

VEGAN MAYONNAISE

PREP + COOK TIME 10 MINUTES
(+ STANDING) MAKES 2 CUPS

Soak 1 cup whole blanched almonds for 4 hours; drain. Rinse under cold water; drain. Blend almonds with ½ cup water until smooth. Add 1 tablespoon apple cider vinegar, 1 tablespoon lemon juice, and 1 teaspoon dijon mustard; blend until smooth and combined. Season to taste. With motor operating, add ½ cup olive oil in a slow, steady stream until smooth and combined. Store in an airtight container in the fridge for up to 1 month.

LEMON & PEPPER

Make vegan mayonnaise opposite; stir in 2 teaspoons finely grated lemon zest and ½ teaspoon ground black pepper.

HARISSA

Make vegan mayonnaise opposite; stir in harissa to taste.

TIPS

If the vegan mayonnaise is not tart enough for your taste, add a little more lemon juice. If it is too tart, add a little cold water.

If possible, try to use a high-speed blender such as a Vitamix to achieve the smoothest consistency.

Spread these vegan mayonnaises on sandwiches, serve as an accompaniment with vegan recipes, as an ingredient in place of egg-based mayonnaise, or as a dip with vegetable sticks.

AÏOLI

Make vegan mayonnaise opposite; stir in 1 clove crushed garlic.

Keralan sweet potato, EGG & FISH CURRY

PREP + COOK TIME 40 MINUTES SERVES 6

1½ pounds firm white fish fillets,
cut into 2-inch pieces

1½ tablespoons ground turmeric

1 medium sweet potato,
halved lengthwise, sliced thickly

2 tablespoons rice bran oil

2 medium yellow onions, sliced thinly

½-ounce piece fresh ginger, cut into matchsticks

¼ cup fresh curry leaves

2 fresh long red chiles, sliced thinly

2 cans (13.5 oz) coconut milk

1 cup water

1 tablespoon tamarind paste

1 tablespoon fish sauce

2 teaspoons lime juice

1 pound packaged brown microwave rice

2 hard-boiled eggs, halved

1 Combine fish and half the turmeric in a medium bowl; refrigerate until required.

2 Meanwhile, boil, steam, or microwave sweet potato until tender; drain.

3 Heat oil in a large saucepan over low heat; cook onion, covered, stirring occasionally, for 5 minutes or until softened (do not brown). Add ginger, 2 tablespoons curry leaves, half the chile, and remaining turmeric; cook, stirring, until fragrant.

4 Add coconut milk, the water, tamarind, fish sauce, and juice; bring to a boil. Add fish and sweet potato; return curry mixture to a boil. Reduce heat; simmer, uncovered, for 3 minutes or until fish is just cooked through.

5 Reheat rice following instructions on package.

6 Top curry with egg, remaining chile, and remaining curry leaves.

tips Good choices of firm white fish for this recipe are pacific john dory, barramundi, ling, and snapper. The curry sauce can be made a day ahead. Reheat the sauce and add raw fish when you are ready to serve.

serving suggestion Serve with steamed jasmine rice.

Seared tuna & QUINOA NIÇOISE SALAD

PREP + COOK TIME 35 MINUTES   SERVES 4

1½ cups red quinoa

4 eggs, at room temperature (see tip)

⅓ pound green beans, trimmed, halved lengthwise

2 tablespoons olive oil

½ pound piece sashimi-grade tuna, skinned

2 tablespoons finely chopped fresh flat-leaf parsley plus ½ cup fresh flat-leaf parsley leaves

1 tablespoon finely chopped fresh chives

½ pound cherry tomatoes, halved

½ cup pitted kalamata olives, halved

CAPER & PARMESAN VINAIGRETTE

1 tablespoon drained baby capers, rinsed, chopped

¼ cup finely grated parmesan

¼ cup white wine vinegar

2 tablespoons olive oil

1 small clove garlic, crushed

1 teaspoon dijon mustard

1 teaspoon superfine sugar

1 Cook quinoa in a large saucepan of boiling water for 12 minutes or until tender; drain. Set aside to cool.
2 Meanwhile, cook eggs in a small saucepan of boiling water for 8 minutes until hard-boiled. Drain; cool eggs under cold running water. Peel.
3 Boil, steam, or microwave beans until tender; drain. Rinse under cold water; drain.
4 Meanwhile, make Caper and Parmesan Vinaigrette.
5 Heat half the oil in a small frying pan over high heat; cook tuna for 1 minute each side or until browned. Slice thinly.
6 Combine chopped parsley and chives in a small bowl. Roll peeled eggs in remaining oil, then herb mixture.
7 Place quinoa and beans in a large bowl with tomatoes, olives, parsley leaves, and vinaigrette; toss to combine. Serve quinoa salad topped with tuna and eggs.
caper & parmesan vinaigrette Combine ingredients in a small bowl; season to taste.

tips If you forget to bring the eggs to room temperature first, place them straight from the fridge into a saucepan of cold water; bring to a boil, then boil for 10 minutes. If you want to "center" the egg yolks, gently stir the eggs until the water comes to a boil.

Vietnamese TURMERIC FISH

PREP + COOK TIME 45 MINUTES (+ STANDING) SERVES 4

This recipe is one of Hanoi's most famous fish dishes.

9 ounces hard tofu, cut into 1¼-inch cubes

½ pound dried rice vermicelli noodles

3 teaspoons ground turmeric

1 teaspoon ground white pepper

½ teaspoon flaky sea salt

¼ cup vegetable oil

¾ pound firm white fish fillets, cut into ¾-inch wide strips

3 shallots, sliced thinly

2 cloves garlic, crushed

1 fresh long red chile, sliced thinly

2 tablespoons grated palm sugar

1 cup water

¼ cup fish sauce

⅔ cup coarsely chopped fresh dill

⅓ cup toasted, salted peanuts, chopped coarsely

1 lime, cut into wedges

1 Place tofu on paper towels; let stand for 30 minutes.

2 Meanwhile, place noodles in a medium heatproof bowl, cover with warm water; let stand for 15 minutes or until just tender. Drain.

3 Combine turmeric, pepper, salt, and 1 tablespoon of the oil in a medium shallow bowl; add tofu and fish, toss gently to coat.

4 Heat remaining oil in a large frying pan over medium-high heat; cook shallots, garlic, and chile until golden. Add sugar; cook, stirring, for 2 minutes or until caramelized.

5 Add the water and fish sauce; bring to a boil. Add ½ cup of the dill and the fish mixture; cook, stirring gently, until fish is just cooked through.

6 Serve fish mixture on noodles, topped with peanuts, remaining dill, and lime wedges.

tip Ling was used in this recipe but you can use any firm white fish you prefer, such as snapper or halibut.

Spanish-style fish
WITH SMOKY EGGPLANT

PREP + COOK TIME 55 MINUTES   SERVES 4

4 eggplants

1 medium red bell pepper

1 teaspoon smoked paprika

2 tablespoons olive oil

8 whiting fillets (about 2 lb)

1 can (15 oz) cannellini beans, drained, rinsed

½ cup mayonnaise

1 clove garlic, crushed

1 tablespoon lemon juice

1 medium lemon, cut into wedges

2 tablespoons coarsely chopped fresh flat-leaf parsley

1 Preheat oven to 400°F. Line a baking sheet with parchment paper.

2 Cut eggplants in half lengthwise; score the flesh. Quarter bell pepper; discard seeds and membranes. Place eggplants and bell pepper, skin-side up, on the baking sheet. Roast for 30 minutes or until bell pepper skin blisters and blackens and eggplant is tender. Transfer to a heatproof bowl; cover with plastic wrap for 5 minutes, then peel away vegetable skins. Shred eggplant coarsely; chop bell pepper coarsely. Season to taste.

3 Meanwhile, combine smoked paprika and half the oil in a medium shallow bowl; add fish, turn to coat. Heat a large non-stick frying pan over high heat; cook fish, in two batches, skin-side first, for 1½ minutes each side or until just cooked through. Transfer to a plate; cover to keep warm.

4 Heat remaining oil in same pan over medium heat; cook beans, stirring, until warmed through. Season to taste.

5 Meanwhile, combine mayonnaise, garlic, and juice in a small bowl; season to taste.

6 Serve fish with eggplant, bell pepper, beans, aïoli, and lemon wedges; top with parsley.

Spicy salmon MIXED-GRAIN SUSHI

PREP + COOK TIME 1 HOUR (+ STANDING & REFRIGERATION) SERVES 6

½ cup brown rice

¼ cup tri-color quinoa

¼ cup pearl barley

2 cups water

¼ cup rice vinegar

2 tablespoons superfine sugar

½ teaspoon flaky sea salt

¼ cup sunflower seeds, chopped finely

2 sheets toasted seaweed (nori)

⅓ pound sashimi-grade salmon, sliced thinly

½ teaspoon chili powder

1 medium avocado, sliced thinly

1 teaspoon lemon juice

PICKLED CUCUMBER

2 persian cucumbers, peeled, sliced thinly

2 tablespoons rice vinegar

1 tablespoon superfine sugar

1 clove garlic, sliced thinly

1 Bring rice, quinoa, barley, and the water to a boil in a medium saucepan. Reduce heat; simmer, covered, for 30 minutes or until water is absorbed. Remove from heat; let stand, covered, for 10 minutes.

2 Meanwhile, combine vinegar, sugar, and salt in a small bowl. Place rice mixture and seeds in a large, wide, stainless steel bowl. Using a plastic spatula, repeatedly slice through rice mixture at an angle to separate grains, gradually pouring in vinegar mixture. Let stand for 10 minutes to cool.

3 Grease and line an 8-inch square cake pan with plastic wrap. Place one nori sheet, trimming to fit, shiny side-down, over base of pan. Spread half the rice mixture over nori. Top with salmon; sprinkle with chili powder.

4 Combine avocado and juice in a small bowl. Place avocado mixture over salmon; top with remaining rice mixture. Place remaining nori sheet, trimming to fit, shiny side-up, over rice mixture. Cover nori with plastic wrap. Place food cans on sushi to weight it down. Refrigerate for 6 hours or until firm enough to cut.

5 Make pickled cucumber.

6 Remove sushi from pan; cut into squares. Serve with Pickled Cucumber.

pickled cucumber Combine ingredients in a medium bowl; let stand for 5 minutes for flavors to develop. Drain.

serving suggestion Serve with soy sauce and wasabi.

VEG IT UP!
REPLACE THE FISH WITH
A THIN PLAIN OMELET
OR SLICES OF
MARINATED TOFU

VEG IT UP!
USE EGGPLANT OR
SWEET POTATO INSTEAD OF
THE FISH.

Fish skewers with labne & CHILE TOMATO SALAD

PREP + COOK TIME 30 MINUTES SERVES 4

¾ pound firm white fish fillets,
cut into 1-inch pieces

1 tablespoon garlic oil

½ teaspoon sumac

9 ounces labne

2 tablespoons toasted sliced almonds

CHILE TOMATO SALAD

¾ pound mixed baby heirloom tomatoes, chopped coarsely

1 tablespoon thinly sliced preserved lemon rind

1 fresh long red chile, seeded, sliced thinly

1 cup fresh flat-leaf parsley leaves

½ cup fresh mint leaves

2 tablespoons red wine vinegar

1 tablespoon garlic oil

1 Place fish and oil in a medium bowl; toss to coat. Thread fish onto four skewers; season.

2 Heat a large non-stick frying pan over high heat; cook fish for 3 minutes each side or until just cooked through. Sprinkle with sumac.

3 Meanwhile, make Chile Tomato Salad.

4 Serve fish on salad with labne; top with almonds.

chile tomato salad Place ingredients in a large bowl; toss gently to combine. Season to taste.

tips You can use any firm white fish you prefer for this recipe. Preserved lemon is available at Middle Eastern markets and well-stocked supermarkets. Remove and discard the flesh, rinse the rind, then use it as the recipe directs. You could use 2 teaspoons finely grated lemon zest instead.

Meat-free MONDAYS

For the meat eater who sees the benefit in giving vegetarian food a go, one day a week.
These recipes contain dairy and eggs.

Zucchini, black bean & CORN ENCHILADAS

PREP + COOK TIME 1 HOUR 40 MINUTES   SERVES 4

3 large zucchini

⅓ cup olive oil

2 trimmed ears of corn

8 x 8-inch white corn tortillas

1 can (15 oz) black beans, drained, rinsed

½ cup fresh cilantro leaves

3 ounces feta

¼ cup fresh oregano leaves

ENCHILADA SAUCE

1 large can (28 oz) crushed tomatoes

1½ cups vegetable stock (see page 40)

2 tablespoons olive oil

2 tablespoon coarsely chopped fresh oregano

2 tablespoon apple cider vinegar

1 medium yellow onion, chopped coarsely

1 clove garlic, chopped

1 tablespoon chopped pickled jalapeños

1 teaspoon ground cumin

1 teaspoon superfine sugar

¼ teaspoon ground chili powder

1 Preheat oven to 350°F. Line a baking sheet with parchment paper. Grease a 10-inch x 12-inch ovenproof dish.
2 Cut zucchini in half lengthwise, then cut each half into long thin wedges. Place zucchini on baking sheet; drizzle with half the oil. Roast 30 minutes or until just tender; chop coarsely.
3 Meanwhile make Enchilada Sauce.
4 Brush corn with 1 tablespoon of the oil. Heat a grill pan over medium-high heat; cook corn, turning occasionally, for 10 minutes or until golden and tender. Using a sharp knife, cut kernels from cobs; discard cobs.
5 Reheat grill pan over medium-high heat; cook tortillas for 30 seconds each side or until lightly charred. Transfer to a plate; cover to keep warm.
6 Combine zucchini, beans, cilantro, half the corn, half the feta, half the oregano, and ½ cup enchilada sauce in a large bowl.
7 Divide zucchini filling evenly among warm tortillas; roll to enclose filling. Place tortillas in dish; brush tops with remaining oil. Spoon remaining Enchilada Sauce over tortillas, leaving ¾ inch at each end of enchiladas uncovered. Top with remaining feta and oregano.
8 Bake for 30 minutes or until golden and heated through. Serve topped with remaining corn and extra oregano.
enchilada sauce Blend or process ingredients until smooth; transfer to a medium saucepan. Bring to a simmer over medium heat for 20 minutes or until thickened slightly.

Cauliflower 'pizza'
WITH MOZZARELLA & ZUCCHINI

PREP + COOK TIME 1 HOUR 25 MINUTES SERVES 4

1 small cauliflower, trimmed, cut into florets

¼ cup coarsely grated cheddar

1 egg, beaten lightly

¾ cup coarsely grated parmesan

½ cup tomato sauce

2 small zucchini, sliced thinly into ribbons

1 cup fresh basil leaves

1 fresh small red (serrano) chile, sliced thinly

3 ounces buffalo mozzarella, torn coarsely

1 tablespoon olive oil

1 tablespoon finely grated lemon zest or strips (see tips)

1 tablespoon lemon juice

1 Preheat oven to 400°F. Line two baking sheets with parchment paper; mark an 8¾-inch round on paper, turn paper over.

2 Process cauliflower until finely chopped. Place in a microwave-safe bowl, cover with plastic wrap; microwave on high (100%) for 12 minutes or until tender. (Alternatively, steam cauliflower, but do not boil it as this will make the crust too soggy). Drain. When cool enough to handle, place cauliflower in the center of a clean kitchen towel. Gather ends together, then squeeze excess moisture from cauliflower.

3 Combine cauliflower, cheddar, egg, and ¼ cup of the parmesan in a large bowl; season. Shape cauliflower mixture into marked rounds on baking sheets; smooth the surface. Bake for 25 minutes or until golden.

4 Spread bases with sauce, half each of the zucchini and basil, then chile, mozzarella, and remaining parmesan. Bake for 20 minutes or until golden and crisp.

5 Meanwhile, combine oil, zest, juice, and remaining zucchini and basil in a medium bowl; season to taste.

6 Serve pizzas topped with zucchini salad.

tips Use a zester to create strips of lemon zest. If you don't have one, peel two long, wide strips of rind from the lemon, without the white pith, then cut them lengthwise into thin strips.

Spiced lentil &
SWEET POTATO PIES

PREP + COOK TIME 1 HOUR 20 MINUTES (+ COOLING) MAKES 8

2 tablespoons olive oil

1 medium red onion, chopped finely

3 cloves garlic, chopped finely

1 celery stalk, trimmed, chopped finely

2 tablespoons harissa (see tips)

1 teaspoon ground cumin

1 teaspoon ground coriander

2¼ cups french-style green lentils

2 small sweet potatoes, cut into 1¼-inch pieces

2 cups vegetable stock (see page 40)

½ cup water

¾ pound cherry tomatoes, halved

2 ounces baby spinach leaves

½ cup fresh flat-leaf parsley leaves

½ cup fresh cilantro leaves

1½ teaspoons finely grated lemon zest

4 sheets puff pastry

1 egg, beaten lightly

HERB & LEMON YOGURT

1 cup Greek-style yogurt

¼ cup coarsely chopped fresh flat-leaf parsley

¼ cup coarsely chopped fresh cilantro

1 tablespoon finely chopped preserved lemon peel

1 tablespoon lemon juice

1 Heat oil in a large saucepan over medium heat; cook onion, garlic, and celery for 5 minutes or until onion softens. Add harissa, cumin, and ground coriander, cook, stirring, for 1 minute or until fragrant. Add lentils, sweet potato, stock, and the water; bring to a boil. Reduce heat, simmer, covered, for 20 minutes or until lentils and sweet potato are tender.

2 Add tomatoes; return to a simmer, cook, uncovered, for 5 minutes or until thickened. Stir in spinach, parsley, fresh cilantro, and zest; season to taste; cool.

3 Meanwhile, make Herb and Lemon Yogurt.

4 Preheat oven to 400°F. Grease eight 1 cup pie tins (with a base measurement of 3 inches and a top measurement of 5 inches).

5 Cut eight 5¼-inch squares from pastry. Refrigerate until required.

6 Fill pie tins with cooled lentil filling; top with pastry squares, pressing edges to seal. Brush tops with egg. Cut small steam holes in top of pies.

7 Bake pies for 30 minutes or until pastry is golden and filling is hot. Serve with Herb and Lemon Yogurt.

herb & lemon yogurt Combine ingredients in a bowl.

tips Harissa is a hot chile paste; there are many different brands available on the market, and the strengths vary enormously. If you have a low heat-level tolerance, you may find this, and any other recipe containing harissa, too hot to tolerate, even if you reduce the amount. Preserved lemon is available at Middle Eastern markets and some supermarkets. Remove and discard the flesh, wash the peel, then use it as the recipe directs.

VEGAN!
USE A VEGAN PUFF
PASTRY AND OMIT THE EGG.
USE SOY YOGURT OR
MAKE VEGAN YOGURT
ON PAGE 210.

Roasted STICKY TOFU BUNS

PREP + COOK TIME 45 MINUTES (+ STANDING)   SERVES 4

9 ounces firm tofu

1 teaspoon smoked paprika

1½ tablespoons ketchup

1½ tablespoons smoky barbecue sauce

¼ cup soy sauce

¼ cup plus 2 tablespoons rice wine vinegar

2 tablespoons brown sugar

1 persian cucumber, sliced thinly lengthwise

1 large carrot, sliced thinly lengthwise

1 fresh long red chile, sliced thinly on the diagonal

1 tablespoon superfine sugar

4 fresh cilantro sprigs

1 tablespoon coarsely chopped toasted salted peanuts

4 small soft white bread rolls, split

1 Preheat oven to 400°F. Grease and line a baking sheet with parchment paper.

2 Place tofu on a plate lined with paper towels. Top with another plate; let stand for 10 minutes. Cut tofu crosswise into eight slices, rub with paprika; season.

3 Bring sauces, ¼ cup vinegar, and sugar to a simmer in a small saucepan over medium heat. Simmer for 3 minutes or until thickened slightly. Pour sauce mixture over tofu; turn to coat. Transfer tofu to baking sheet; bake for 20 minutes, basting occasionally with sauce mixture or until tofu is golden.

4 Combine cucumber, carrot, chile, sugar, and remaining vinegar in a medium bowl; let stand for 10 minutes or until vegetables soften. Drain.

5 Place tofu, pickled vegetables, cilantro, and nuts between rolls.

tip This recipe can easily be doubled or tripled to feed more people.

Root vegetable
PAN PIZZA

PREP + COOK TIME 1 HOUR (+ STANDING) SERVES 6

4 x 2-inch fresh rosemary sprigs

2 cloves garlic, crushed

2 teaspoons fresh thyme leaves

⅓ cup olive oil

4 small potatoes, unpeeled, scrubbed, sliced thinly

1 small orange sweet potato, unpeeled, scrubbed, sliced thinly

1 small parsnip, unpeeled, scrubbed, sliced thinly lengthwise

¼ pound baby carrots, unpeeled, scrubbed, trimmed

1 cup firmly packed trimmed watercress

2 teaspoons finely grated lemon zest

1 teaspoon lemon juice

1 ounce feta, crumbled

WHOLE-GRAIN PIZZA DOUGH

2¼ teaspoons active dried yeast

1 teaspoon superfine sugar

1 cup warm water, approximately

1½ cups bread flour or all-purpose flour

1½ cups whole-grain all-purpose flour

1 teaspoon salt

¼ cup olive oil

1 Make Whole-Grain Pizza Dough.

2 Preheat oven to 425°F. Grease an 11¼-inch x 12¾-inch baking sheet.

3 Remove leaves from rosemary sprigs; finely chop two-thirds of the leaves. Combine chopped rosemary, garlic, thyme, and 2 tablespoons of the oil in a small bowl.

4 Turn dough onto floured surface; knead until smooth. Flatten dough; roll to an 11¼-inch x 12¾-inch rectangle. Carefully lift onto baking sheet; spread rosemary mixture over base, leaving a ¾-inch border. Top with a layer of potato, sweet potato, parsnip, and carrots; sprinkle with whole rosemary leaves. Season. Drizzle with 1 tablespoon of the oil.

5 Bake pizza for 20 minutes or until base is browned and crisp.

6 Meanwhile, combine watercress, 2 teaspoons of the oil, zest, and juice in a medium bowl; season to taste.

7 Drizzle pizza with remaining oil; top with feta and watercress salad.

whole-grain pizza dough Combine yeast, sugar, and the warm water in a small bowl; let stand in a warm place for 10 minutes or until mixture is frothy. Combine flours and salt in a large bowl; stir in yeast mixture and oil, to a soft dough. Knead dough on a floured surface for 5 minutes or until smooth and elastic. Place dough in a large oiled bowl, cover; let stand in a warm place for 1 hour or until dough has doubled in size.

tip Use a mandoline or V-slicer to slice the vegetables very thinly.

Pumpkin gnocchi
WITH BROCCOLINI & RED ONION

PREP + COOK TIME 30 MINUTES SERVES 4

Green cruciferous vegetables such as broccolini are an important part of any diet, offering a wide array of cancer-preventing nutrients and antioxidants. Broccoli and kale, vegetables in the same family, can be substituted.

1 pound pumpkin gnocchi

1 tablespoon olive oil

2 medium red onions, cut into six wedges

¼ cup butter

1 clove garlic, crushed

2 teaspoons fresh thyme leaves

⅓ pound broccolini, halved crosswise

1½ ounces soft goat cheese, crumbled

1 Cook gnocchi in a large saucepan of boiling water, uncovered, until just tender. Drain, reserving ¾ cup of the cooking liquid. Place gnocchi in a single layer on a baking sheet.

2 Meanwhile, heat oil in a large frying pan over low heat; cook onion, stirring occasionally, until softened. Remove from pan.

3 Reheat same pan over high heat with half the butter, add half the gnocchi; cook, tossing, for 3 minutes or until golden. Remove from pan. Repeat with remaining butter and gnocchi.

4 Reheat same pan over medium heat, return onion to pan with garlic, thyme, and broccolini; cook, stirring, until broccolini is almost tender. Return gnocchi to pan, with enough of the reserved cooking liquid to coat; season to taste. Serve gnocchi topped with goat cheese.

tip Instead of adding the cooking liquid in step 4, add ⅔ cup cream to the pan with the broccolini.

Squash & feta FREEFORM TART

PREP + COOK TIME 1 HOUR 30 MINUTES (+ REFRIGERATION) SERVES 4

1½ pounds kabocha squash, cut into
1¼-inch pieces

2 medium red onions, cut into wedges

2 teaspoons fresh thyme leaves

1 tablespoon olive oil

3 ounces feta, crumbled

2 bocconcini, torn

2 tablespoons fresh thyme

CREAM CHEESE PASTRY

1¼ cups all-purpose flour

½ teaspoon flaky sea salt

4 ounces cold cream cheese, chopped

1 egg

1 tablespoon cold water, approximately

MIXED LEAF SALAD

3 ounces baby mesclun

½ cup coarsely chopped fresh flat-leaf parsley

1 tablespoon fresh dill sprigs

1 medium bosc pear, cut into matchsticks

1 tablespoon olive oil

1 tablespoon lemon juice

1 Preheat oven to 400°F. Line a baking sheet with parchment paper.

2 Place squash, onion, and thyme on baking sheet; drizzle with oil. Season. Bake for 25 minutes or until tender. Cool.

3 Meanwhile, make Cream Cheese Pastry.

4 Roll pastry between sheets of parchment paper to a 12-inch round. Remove top sheet of parchment paper; lift pastry on paper to a second baking sheet. Top pastry with squash mixture, feta, and bocconcini, leaving a 1½-inch border all around. Fold pastry side over filling, pleating as you go to partially cover.

5 Bake tart for 30 minutes or until golden and base is cooked through.

6 Meanwhile, make Mixed Leaf Salad.

7 Serve tart topped with thyme and with salad.

cream cheese pastry Process flour, salt, and cream cheese until crumbly; add egg and the water, pulse until mixture just comes together. Knead dough on a floured surface until smooth. Wrap in plastic wrap; refrigerate for 20 minutes.

mixed leaf salad Place ingredients in a large bowl; toss gently to combine. Season to taste.

If you're getting bored with the same old same old, up the tempo with a spice mix. Some of our global favorites include:

Za'atar A Middle Eastern mix of sumac, sesame seeds, and thyme. Try with baked eggs, breads, green veggies, grains, and pulses.

Ras al hanout Another Middle Eastern mix that can be made of up to 22 spices. It is perfect in a vegetable tagine, lentil dishes, or tossed with wedges of squash.

Togarashi A Japanese mix of seaweed, tangerine rind, sesame seeds, and chile. Sprinkle on veggie soups, omelets, rice dishes, or avocado on toast.

Panch phoron Less wellknown than India's famous garam masala. Unlike garam masala, this Bengali mix contains the seeds of fenugreek, nigella, black mustard, fennel, and cumin. Fry in ghee or coconut oil and stir through potatoes, sweet potato, green beans, or raita.

FOOD
for thought

YOU CAN REDUCE YOUR SHOPPING FOOTPRINT BY CHOOSING LOOSE FRUITS AND VEGETABLES OVER PRE-PACKAGED ONES ON POLYSTYRENE TRAYS. ALSO, INCREASINGLY GROCERS ARE SELLING NUTS, SEEDS, AND GRAINS FROM DISPENSERS, GIVING THE CONSUMER THE CHOICE OF BUYING AS LITTLE OR AS MUCH AS THEY NEED.

FIVE THINGS TO MAKE WITH LEFTOVER BREAD:

PANZANELLA

Cut bread into large chunks, drizzle with olive oil, and toss with 2 flattened cloves of garlic; roast until golden. Toss with a salad of ripe tomatoes, roasted bell pepper, cucumber, olives and capers.

FRESH BREAD CRUMBS

Cut bread and the crust into chunks; process, in batches, into coarse or fine crumbs. Pack into small bags, freeze until required. Use crumbs to coat egg-dipped zucchini, eggplant, or asparagus before cooking.

SAVORY PUDDING

Layer slices of bread in individual ovenproof dishes with leftover roasted squash. Whisk 4 eggs with 3 cups milk, add grated parmesan, a little chopped sage or thyme, and bake (see also recipe on page 31).

BRUSCHETTA

Brush slices of bread with olive oil, then grill until both sides are lightly toasted; rub one side with garlic and top with fried mushrooms and creamed kale.

PANGRATTATO

Tear bread into pieces, drizzle with olive oil and sprinkle with red pepper flakes; toast in a frying pan or in the oven. Sprinkle over chargrilled asparagus or toss through pasta.

SO YOU THOUGHT THE CARDBOARD PIZZA BOX WAS RECYCLABLE? WELL, YES AND NO. THE BOX ITSELF IS, BUT ONCE THE CARDBOARD BECOMES SOILED WITH CHEESE AND GREASE, IT'S NOT.

WASTE NOT *want not*

LEFTOVERS

turn roasted vegetables into hash Heat extra-virgin oil olive in a pan with sliced garlic, fennel seeds, and a little chile, toss the coarsely chopped vegetables until lightly browned and hot. Stir in a few peas or add kernels from a cob of corn; roll up in grainy flatbreads with a little fresh milky mozzarella and toasted nuts.

turn cooked green vegies into a pizza Layer and stack lavash wraps with a little parmesan; spread with a thin layer of ricotta, top with leftover cooked green vegetables, red pepper flakes, and grated lemon rind. Bake in a preheated 350°F oven until bread is crisp. Serve drizzled with olive oil.

turn pasta into a frittata Beat 6 eggs, add leftover pasta, ½ cup pecorino, and 1½ cups crushed thawed frozen peas. Cook an onion in a medium frying pan, add pasta mixture to pan; cook until almost set. Place frittata under the broiler to finish off the cooking.

Packaging

As a general rule, the smaller the packaging and the greater the mix of blended materials in packaging, the less suitable it is for recycling. Plastics in particular are problematic; while many may be stamped with a recyclable symbol, they aren't. You can contact your local agency to find out what they are able to process.

Thai YELLOW CURRY

PREP + COOK TIME 1 HOUR SERVES 4

1 tablespoon rice bran oil

1 medium red onion, sliced thinly

¼ cup yellow curry paste

2 cloves garlic, crushed

4-inch stick fresh lemongrass, bruised

4 fresh kaffir lime leaves, shredded finely

1⅔ cups coconut milk

1 cup water

1½ pounds sweet potato, unpeeled, scrubbed, chopped coarsely

6½ ounces green beans, trimmed

½ pound assorted mushrooms

1 tablespoon finely grated palm sugar

1 tablespoon fish sauce (see tip)

2 tablespoons lime juice

1 fresh long red chile, seeded, sliced thinly

¼ cup fried shallots

½ cup fresh thai basil leaves

1 Heat oil in a wok or large saucepan over high heat; cook onion, stirring, for 5 minutes or until onion softens. Add paste, garlic, lemongrass, and kaffir lime leaves; cook, stirring, for 1 minute or until fragrant.
2 Add coconut milk, the water, and sweet potatoes; bring to a boil. Reduce heat, simmer, uncovered, for 20 minutes or until sweet potato is just tender. Stir in beans and mushrooms; cook, uncovered, for 5 minutes or until vegetables are tender. Stir in sugar, sauce, and juice; remove and discard lemongrass.
3 Serve curry sprinkled with chile, shallots, and basil.

tip If you are avoiding all animal derived products, use tamari instead of the fish sauce.

Chile beans
WITH CHIMICHURRI

PREP + COOK TIME 1 HOUR SERVES 4

2 chipotle chiles

½ cup boiling water

1 tablespoon olive oil

1 large yellow onion, chopped finely

2 teaspoons ground cumin

2 teaspoons ground coriander

1 teaspoon mexican chili powder

1 can (15 oz) red kidney beans, drained, rinsed

1 can (15 oz) chickpeas (garbanzo beans), drained, rinsed

2 cans (14.5 oz each) diced tomatoes

¼ cup water

½ cup fresh cilantro sprigs

¼ cup sour cream

TORTILLA CHIPS

4 x 6¾-inch white corn tortillas, quartered

cooking oil spray

½ teaspoon sweet paprika

CHIMICHURRI

½ small red onion, chopped finely

1 clove garlic, chopped finely

½ teaspoon sweet paprika

½ cup olive oil

1½ tablespoons red wine vinegar

½ cup finely chopped fresh flat-leaf parsley

2 tablespoons finely chopped fresh oregano

1 Place chiles in a small heatproof bowl, cover with the boiling water; let stand 20 minutes. Coarsely chop chiles; discard stems. Blend or process chopped chiles with soaking liquid until smooth.

2 Meanwhile, make the Tortilla Chips, then Chimichurri.

3 Heat oil in a large saucepan over medium heat; cook onion, stirring, for 5 minutes or until onion softens. Add cumin, ground coriander, and chili powder; cook, stirring, for 1 minute or until fragrant.

4 Add beans, chickpeas, chipotle mixture, tomatoes, and the water; bring to a boil. Reduce heat; cook for 15 minutes or until sauce thickens.

5 Serve chile beans topped with chimichurri and fresh cilantro, and with tortilla chips and sour cream.

tortilla chips Preheat oven to 400°F. Spray tortillas with oil; sprinkle with paprika. Place on a baking sheet; bake for 5 minutes or until crisp.

chimichurri Combine ingredients in a small bowl; season to taste.

tip Chipotle chiles are dried jalapeño chiles; they are available from spice shops and markets. Substitute with 1 teaspoon smoked paprika and increase mexican chili powder to 2 teaspoons.

serving suggestion Serve with guacamole and lime wedges.

Carrot & harissa
FALAFEL WITH TAHINI YOGURT

PREP + COOK TIME 1 HOUR SERVES 4

2 medium carrots, grated coarsely

1 can (15 oz) chickpeas (garbanzo beans), drained, rinsed

1 small red onion, chopped finely

1 teaspoon ground cumin

1 tablespoon harissa

¼ cup all-purpose flour

½ teaspoon baking powder

1 free-range egg

1½ cups panko (japanese) bread crumbs

vegetable oil, for deep-frying

¼ pound green beans, trimmed, halved lengthwise

2 heads baby romaine lettuce, leaves separated

1 persian cucumber, sliced thinly

¼ cup fresh flat-leaf parsley leaves

2 teaspoons lemon zest strips (see tip)

TAHINI YOGURT

1 small clove garlic, crushed

2 tablespoons lemon juice

2 tablespoons tahini

¾ cup Greek-style yogurt

1 tablespoon shredded fresh flat-leaf parsley

1 Process carrots, chickpeas, onion, cumin, harissa, flour, baking powder, and egg until mixture just comes together; season. Transfer mixture to a large bowl; stir in ¾ cup of the bread crumbs. Roll level tablespoons of carrot mixture into balls (mixture should make about 28). Roll falafel in remaining bread crumbs to coat.

2 Fill a large saucepan or wok one-third with oil and heat to 350°F (or until a cube of bread browns in 15 seconds). Deep-fry falafel, in batches, for 2 minutes or until golden and cooked through. Drain on paper towels.

3 Meanwhile, make Tahini Yogurt.

4 Boil, steam, or microwave beans until just tender; drain. Rinse under cold water; drain.

5 Combine lettuce, cucumber, and beans in a large bowl. Serve salad topped with falafel and tahini yogurt; sprinkle with parsley and lemon zest.

tahini yogurt Combine ingredients in small bowl; season to taste.

tip If you have one, use a zester to create the strips of lemon zest. If you don't have one, peel two long, wide strips of zest from the lemon, without the white pith, then cut them lengthwise into thin strips.

Rice cakes with ZUCCHINI & MUSHROOMS

PREP + COOK TIME 1 HOUR SERVES 4

3 cups brown rice, rinsed

5 cups water

1 tablespoon mirin

2 tablespoons light soy sauce

1 teaspoon superfine sugar

¼ cup rice vinegar

2½ tablespoons sesame oil

2 green onions, sliced thinly

¼ pound shiitake mushrooms, sliced thickly

¼ pound shimeji mushrooms, separated

2 medium zucchini, cut into matchsticks

¼ pound snow peas, trimmed

1 sheet toasted seaweed (nori), sliced thinly

1 Bring rice and the water to a boil in a large saucepan over medium-high heat. Reduce heat; simmer, covered, for 30 minutes or until rice is just tender. Remove from heat; let stand, covered, until cool enough to handle.

2 Meanwhile, combine mirin, sauce, sugar, vinegar, and 2 teaspoons of the oil in a small bowl; set aside.

3 Place half the rice, half the white part of the green onions, and 1 teaspoon of the oil in a food processor; pulse until rice is coarsely chopped and sticky. Transfer rice mixture to a large bowl. Repeat with remaining rice, white part of the green onions, and another 1 teaspoon of oil. Stir rice mixture to combine. Shape rice mixture into 16 patties. Brush rice cakes with 1 tablespoon of the oil.

4 Heat a large frying pan over medium heat; cook rice cakes, in batches, for 5 minutes each side or until golden and crisp.

5 Meanwhile, heat remaining oil in a wok or large frying pan over medium-high heat; cook mushrooms until almost tender. Add zucchini and peas; cook for 1 minute or until tender. Add mirin mixture; toss to combine.

6 Serve rice cakes with stir-fried vegetables, sprinkled with seaweed and remaining green onion.

Crisp cheese ravioli
WITH SALSA VERDE

PREP + COOK TIME 45 MINUTES   SERVES 6

Pan-fried ravioli is such a textural treat with a crisp exterior and molten cheese center. We've paired it with a zingy herb sauce to cut through the richness.

4 ounces buffalo mozzarella

2 cups coarsely grated provolone cheese

36 round gow gee wrappers

5 eggs, beaten lightly

3 cups panko (japanese) bread crumbs

vegetable oil, for shallow-frying

⅓ pound asparagus, trimmed, sliced thinly lengthwise (see tip)

SALSA VERDE

2 cups fresh mint leaves, chopped coarsely

2 cups fresh basil leaves, chopped coarsely

1 tablespoon drained capers, chopped finely

1 clove garlic, chopped finely

¼ cup olive oil

¼ cup lemon juice

2 tablespoons water

1 Drain mozzarella; pat dry with paper towels, then chop coarsely. Combine mozzarella and provolone in a medium bowl; season. Place 1 tablespoon of cheese mixture in the center of one wrapper; brush around edges with a little water. Top with another wrapper; press edges together to seal. Repeat with remaining cheese mixture and wrappers.

2 Cook ravioli in a large saucepan of boiling water for 1 minute or until just tender; drain. Transfer to a baking sheet lined with paper towels; set aside to cool.

3 Meanwhile, make Salsa Verde.

4 Carefully dip ravioli in egg, then coat in bread crumbs. Heat ¾-inch oil in a large deep frying pan; cook ravioli, in batches, for 1 minute each side or until golden and crisp. Drain on paper towels.

5 Serve ravioli with asparagus and salsa verde.

salsa verde Process ingredients until finely chopped; season to taste.

tip We used a vegetable peeler to slice the asparagus into long thin ribbons. Alternatively, blanch asparagus ribbons for a few seconds in boiling water.

Semolina gnocchi
WITH MUSHROOM RAGU

PREP + COOK TIME 1 HOUR 10 MINUTES (+ REFRIGERATION) SERVES 4

¾ ounce dried porcini mushrooms

1½ cups boiling water

3 cups milk

3 tablespoons butter, chopped coarsely

¼ cup olive oil

1 cup fine semolina

2 egg yolks

1 cup finely grated parmesan

2 shallots, chopped finely

2 cloves garlic, chopped finely

½ pound cremini mushrooms, sliced thickly

2 portobello mushrooms, cut into wedges

2 tablespoons fresh thyme leaves

1 can (14.5 oz) diced tomatoes

¼ cup fresh flat-leaf parsley leaves

1 Grease an 8-inch x 12-inch x 1¼-inch baking pan.

2 Place porcini mushrooms in a small heatproof bowl with the boiling water; let stand 10 minutes. Drain; reserve soaking liquid.

3 Bring milk, butter, and 1 tablespoon of the oil to a boil in a large saucepan over high heat; gradually whisk in semolina. Reduce heat; whisk continuously for 15 minutes or until semolina thickens. Remove from heat. Add egg yolks and ¾ cup of the parmesan; stir until cheese melts. Pour mixture into pan; cool. Refrigerate for 30 minutes or until firm.

4 Meanwhile, heat remaining oil in a large frying pan over medium-high heat; cook shallots, garlic, fresh mushrooms, and thyme, stirring, for 8 minutes or until tender. Add tomatoes, porcini, and reserved soaking liquid; cook for 5 minutes or until thickened slightly. Season to taste.

5 Preheat broiler. Line a baking sheet with foil.

6 Cut semolina into 12 rectangles; place on baking sheet, then sprinkle with remaining parmesan. Broil for 5 minutes or until golden and heated through. Serve semolina gnocchi topped with mushroom ragu and parsley.

Spinach, cheese & POTATO CANNELLONI

PREP + COOK TIME 1 HOUR 35 MINUTES SERVES 6

1¼ pounds potatoes, chopped coarsely

1 pound spinach, trimmed, chopped coarsely

6 ounces feta, crumbled

1 cup finely grated pecorino cheese or parmesan

3 cloves garlic, chopped finely

2 tablespoons finely chopped fresh sage

¼ cup olive oil

1 large can (28 oz) tomato sauce

2 teaspoons raw sugar

1 can (14.5 oz) diced tomatoes

¼ cup water

½ pound dried no-boil cannelloni tubes

1 Place potatoes in a large saucepan with enough cold water to just cover; bring to a boil. Boil for 15 minutes or until potato is tender; drain. Mash potato in a large bowl; season to taste.

2 Meanwhile, boil, steam or microwave spinach until wilted; drain. When cool enough to handle, squeeze excess water from spinach.

3 Add spinach to mashed potato with 4½ ounces feta, ⅔ cup pecorino, garlic, and sage; season to taste.

4 Place oil, tomato sauce, sugar, tomatoes, and the water in a large saucepan over medium heat; bring to a boil. Reduce heat; simmer for 10 minutes or until reduced slightly.

5 Meanwhile, preheat oven to 350°F.

6 Using a large piping bag, fill cannelloni with potato mixture. Spread ½ cup sauce into a shallow 10-inch x 12¾-inch ovenproof dish; top with cannelloni, in a single layer, then top with remaining sauce, feta, and pecorino. Cover dish with foil.

7 Bake cannelloni for 30 minutes or until pasta is tender. Increase oven to 400°F, remove foil from dish; cook for a further 10 minutes or until golden.

BAKED VEGETABLE CHIPS
PREP + COOK TIME 1 HOUR 30 MINUTES **SERVES** 2

Preheat oven to 300°F. Line three baking sheets with parchment paper, then coat with cooking oil spray; sprinkle with sea salt flakes. Using a mandoline or V-slicer, cut 1 large carrot, 1 large purple carrot and 1 medium parsnip lengthwise into paper-thin slices. Place vegetables in a single layer on baking sheets. Spray with cooking oil; sprinkle with a little more sea salt flakes (or one of the seasoning variations opposite). Bake for 1¼ hours or until crisp; cool.

SMOKED PAPRIKA

1 teaspoon smoked paprika

SUMAC & THYME

1 teaspoon sumac and 2 teaspoons chopped fresh thyme

FENNEL & RED PEPPER FLAKES

Grind 2 teaspoons fennel seeds with a pestle and mortar until coarsely ground; stir in 1 teaspoon red pepper flakes.

TIPS

Try making chips from other vegetables such as jerusalem artichokes, sweet potato, and white or purple sweet potato.

Store vegetable chips in an airtight container for up to 4 days.

Fennel & chile seasoning can be stored in a well-sealed jar for up to 1 week.

Kale & walnut TARTS

PREP + COOK TIME 1 HOUR 20 MINUTES SERVES 6

3 tablespoons butter, melted

2½ cups LSA (see tips)

6 eggs

1 ounce baby kale leaves, chopped finely

⅓ cup chopped toasted walnuts

⅔ cup ricotta, crumbled

1⅓ cups milk

2 teaspoons finely grated lemon zest

2 cloves garlic, crushed

2 teaspoons finely chopped fresh tarragon

2 ounces snow pea tendrils

1 tablespoon lemon juice

1 tablespoon olive oil

1 Preheat oven to 400°F. Brush six 4-inch loose-based fluted tart tins with half the melted butter. Place tins on a baking sheet.

2 Combine LSA, 2 of the eggs, and remaining melted butter in a medium bowl; season. Press LSA mixture onto base and side of tins. Bake for 10 minutes; set aside to cool. Reduce oven to 325°F.

3 Place kale, walnuts, and ricotta in tart cases. Whisk remaining 4 eggs, milk, zest, garlic, and tarragon in a large jug until combined; season. Pour egg mixture over filling.

4 Bake tarts for 30 minutes or until just set. Leave tarts in tins for 5 minutes to cool slightly, but while still warm, remove from tins (see tips).

5 Meanwhile, combine snow pea tendrils, juice, and oil in a small bowl; season to taste.

6 Serve tarts topped with snow pea tendrils.

tips LSA is a ground linseed (flaxseed), sunflower seed, and almond mixture that can be found at supermarkets and health-food stores. You must remove the tarts from the tins while they are still warm to prevent them from sticking.

Mushroom, sage & BUCKWHEAT RISOTTO

PREP + COOK TIME 1 HOUR   SERVES 4

2 tablespoons plus ¼ cup olive oil

⅓ pound button mushrooms, sliced thinly

¾ pound portobello mushrooms, sliced thinly

1 medium onion, chopped finely

3 cloves garlic, sliced thinly

2 tablespoons chopped fresh sage leaves, plus ⅓ cup whole sage leaves

1½ cups buckwheat

1 cup dry white wine

5 cups vegetable stock (see page 40), warmed

1 cup finely grated parmesan

6 ounces labne (see tips)

⅓ cup toasted sliced almonds

1 Heat 2 tablespoons of the oil in a large saucepan over high heat; cook mushrooms, in two batches, for 10 minutes or until golden. Remove from pan.
2 Reheat remaining oil in same pan over medium heat; cook onion, garlic, and chopped sage for 5 minutes or until onion softens. Add buckwheat; cook, stirring, for 1 minute or until coated. Add wine; cook, stirring, for 1 minute.
3 Add stock; bring to a boil. Reduce heat to low; simmer, uncovered, for 30 minutes, stirring occasionally or until buckwheat is tender. Stir in mushrooms and parmesan; season to taste
4 Meanwhile, heat remaining ¼ cup oil in a small frying pan over medium heat; cook sage leaves for 30 seconds or until crisp. Drain on paper towels.
5 Serve risotto topped with labne, crisp sage, and almonds.

tips Buckwheat is available from health food stores. Labne is a soft fresh cheese made from strained yogurt; generally it is rolled into balls and stored in olive oil. You can use soft goat's cheese if unavailable.

Eggplant parmigiana "MEATBALL" SUBS

PREP + COOK TIME 1 HOUR SERVES 6

1 medium eggplant, peeled, chopped coarsely

2 tablespoons olive oil

1 can (15 oz) chickpeas (garbanzo beans), drained, rinsed

1 small red onion, chopped finely

2 cloves garlic, crushed

1 tablespoon finely chopped fresh rosemary leaves

1¾ cups finely grated parmesan

1½ cups packaged bread crumbs

vegetable oil, for deep-frying

6 long soft bread rolls

1 cup tomato-based pasta sauce

2 ounces baby arugula leaves

2 teaspoons balsamic vinegar

1 Preheat oven to 400°F. Line a baking sheet with parchment paper.

2 Place eggplant on baking sheet; drizzle with olive oil. Roast for 25 minutes or until golden and tender.

3 Process eggplant, chickpeas, onion, garlic, rosemary, and 1 cup of the parmesan until combined; season. Add 1 cup bread crumbs; pulse until combined. Roll level tablespoons of eggplant mixture into 24 balls. Roll eggplant balls in remaining bread crumbs to coat.

4 Heat vegetable oil in a wok or large saucepan; deep-fry eggplant balls, in batches, for 2 minutes or until golden and heated through. Drain on paper towels.

5 Preheat broiler. Cut rolls lengthwise from the top, without cutting all the way through. Spread sides with sauce; top with 4 eggplant balls and sprinkle with remaining ¾ cup parmesan. Broil for 2 minutes or until cheese melts.

6 Combine arugula and vinegar in a small bowl; divide salad between subs.

Cauliflower "couscous"
WITH ROASTED CARROT HUMMUS

PREP + COOK TIME 45 MINUTES SERVES 4

1¾ pounds cauliflower, trimmed, chopped coarsely

1 tablespoon olive oil

2 tablespoons ground cumin

½ teaspoon ground cardamom

⅓ cup coarsely chopped, toasted unsalted pistachios

⅓ cup toasted pine nuts

½ cup pomegranate seeds

1 cup fresh flat-leaf parsley leaves, chopped coarsely

1 cup fresh mint leaves, chopped coarsely

½ cup goldenberries (see tips)

1 tablespoon finely chopped preserved lemon rind

1 medium lemon, cut into wedges

ROASTED CARROT HUMMUS

3 medium carrots, chopped coarsely

2 teaspoons olive oil

1 cup hummus

1 teaspoon finely grated orange rind

1 Make Roasted Carrot Hummus.

2 Meanwhile, process cauliflower until it resembles couscous. Heat oil in a large frying pan or wok over medium heat; cook cauliflower, stirring, for 5 minutes or until tender. Add cumin and cardamom; cook for 1 minute or until fragrant, season to taste.

3 Combine cauliflower mixture, nuts, seeds, parsley, mint, berries, and preserved lemon in a large bowl. Serve topped with hummus and lemon wedges.

roasted carrot hummus Preheat oven to 350°F. Place carrots on a parchment paper–lined baking sheet; drizzle with oil. Roast for 40 minutes or until tender; cool slightly. Blend or process carrots with remaining ingredients until smooth and combined. Season to taste.

tips Goldenberries are dried physalis peruviana or, as they are also known, cape gooseberries. The fresh orange fruit, which is the size of a cherry tomato, is contained in a green paper-like calyx. The dried fruit have a tangy citrus-like taste, and are high in protein (for a fruit), fiber, and antioxidants. If you can't find them, use dried cranberries instead or 1 medium orange, peeled and segmented.

Lebanese roasted SQUASH SALAD

PREP + COOK TIME 1 HOUR 15 MINUTES   SERVES 6

2 tablespoons honey

1 cup walnuts

4 pounds kabocha squash, cut into 1-inch thick wedges

1 large red bell pepper, sliced thickly

1 large red onion, cut into wedges

2 tablespoons olive oil

1 can (15 oz) lentils, drained, rinsed

2 ounces watercress

LEBANESE SPICE MIX

1 teaspoon sweet paprika

1 teaspoon ground cumin

1 teaspoon ground coriander

1 teaspoon ground cardamom

½ teaspoon ground cinnamon

½ teaspoon ground nutmeg

YOGURT DRESSING

½ cup Greek-style yogurt

¼ cup olive oil

1 tablespoon finely grated lemon zest

¼ cup lemon juice

1 tablespoon honey

1 Preheat oven to 400°F. Line three baking sheets with parchment paper.

2 Make Lebanese Spice Mix.

3 Bring honey to a boil in a small frying pan over medium heat. Add walnuts and 1 teaspoon spice mix; toss gently to coat. Transfer to a baking sheet; set aside to cool.

4 Place squash on another baking sheet, and bell pepper and onion on remaining baking sheet. Drizzle with 2 tablespoons oil and remaining spice mix; toss to coat. Bake for 30 minutes or until bell pepper and onion are tender; remove from oven.

5 Meanwhile, make Yogurt Dressing.

6 Serve roasted vegetables with lentils, watercress, nuts, and yogurt dressing.

lebanese spice mix Combine ingredients in a small bowl.

yogurt dressing Combine ingredients in a small bowl; season to taste.

tip Make extra spice mix and store in an airtight container for up to 1 month.

Tempeh BLAT SANDWICH

PREP + COOK TIME 1 HOUR MAKES 4

1 medium avocado, chopped coarsely

1 tablespoon lemon juice

8 slices sourdough bread, toasted

¼ cup mayonnaise

½ teaspoon ground turmeric

1 medium tomato, sliced thinly

1 medium carrot, cut into matchsticks

2 ounces baby arugula leaves

TEMPEH BACON

2 tablespoons tamari

1 tablespoon olive oil

1 tablespoon pure maple syrup

1 teaspoon smoked paprika

1 package (8 oz) tempeh, cut into ½-inch slices

BEET RELISH

3 medium beet, grated coarsely

1 shallot, chopped finely

2 tablespoons pomegranate molasses

1 teaspoon ground allspice

1 teaspoon coriander seeds, crushed

2 tablespoons red wine vinegar

½ cup water

1 tablespoon olive oil

1 Make Tempeh Bacon.

2 Meanwhile, make Beet Relish.

3 Combine avocado and juice in a small bowl; season.

4 Place 4 slices of bread on a board; spread with combined mayonnaise and turmeric. Top with tomato, tempeh bacon, carrot, avocado mixture, arugula, and beet relish. Top with remaining slices of bread.

tempeh bacon Preheat oven to 400°F. Line a baking sheet with parchment paper. Combine tamari, oil, maple syrup, and paprika in a medium bowl. Add tempeh; toss to coat. Place tempeh, in a single layer, on baking sheet. Bake for 20 minutes, turning halfway through cooking, until crisp.

beet relish Place ingredients, except oil, in a small saucepan over high heat. Reduce heat; simmer, uncovered, for 10 minutes or until thickened. Stir in oil; cool.

tips Beet relish makes about 1½ cups. Store leftover relish, covered, in the refrigerator for up to 2 weeks. Beet relish goes well with cheese or in burgers and sandwiches. If pomegranate molasses is not available, combine 1 tablespoon balsamic vinegar and 1 tablespoon superfine sugar.

Kale & spinach
SPANAKOPITAS

PREP + COOK TIME 1 HOUR 30 MINUTES MAKES 6

3 pounds swiss chard, trimmed

¾ pounf green curly kale

¾ pound feta, crumbled

10 green onions, chopped finely

½ cup finely chopped fresh dill

¾ cup finely chopped fresh flat-leaf parsley

2 teaspoons finely grated lemon zest

¼ cup lemon juice

3 eggs, beaten lightly

5 tablespoons butter, melted

2 packages (12 oz each) fresh filo pastry

1 Preheat oven to 350°F.
2 Trim 1½-inches off the stalks ends from swiss chard and kale; discard. Rinse and drain greens, leaving some water clinging. Tear kale leaves from the center stem.
Cut white stalk from swiss chard leaves, cutting into the leaf in a v-shape. Finely chop stems and leaves from greens, keeping them separate.
3 Heat a large saucepan over high heat; cook stems, stirring occasionally, for 10 minutes or until softened. Drain well. Repeat with chopped leaves. When cool enough to handle, squeeze excess water from greens mixture (this will prevent the pies from becoming soggy).

4 Combine greens, feta, onion,s herbs, zest, juice, and eggs in a large bowl; season with freshly ground black pepper.
5 Butter six 2-cup, 4¾-inch x 6¾-inch oval oven dishes. Butter half a sheet of filo pastry, fold in half to make a smaller rectangle; butter top. Place in dish, allowing pastry to overhang edge. Repeat with two more sheets of pastry, stacking them in the dish. You will now have six layers. Place a sixth of the filling into the tin. Brush half a sheet of filo with melted butter, fold in half crosswise, brush with butter, fold in half again; trim to fit the top of the pie. Place over filling, then fold in and scrunch the overhanging pastry. Brush top of pie with a little more melted butter. Repeat to make five more pies.
6 Sprinkle a little water over each pie; this will prevent the pastry from burning. Bake for 45 minutes or until golden.

tips You will need 1 bunch swiss chard and 1 bunch green curly kale for this recipe. Trim the green onions so that they are 11¼ inches long; discard the remainder of the tops. You can make the spanakopitas up to the end of step 5, then put them into freezer bags and freeze for up to 1 month. Cook them from frozen, increasing the cooking time slightly, or until the pastry is golden and the filling is heated through.
serving suggestion Serve with snow pea tendrils.

Japanese
CABBAGE PANCAKES

PREP + COOK TIME 50 MINUTES (+ STANDING) SERVES 4

These quick Japanese pancakes are known as okonomiyaki. You can easily add extra left over vegetables to the mix if you like.

1¾ cups all-purpose flour

⅓ cup cornstarch

2 eggs

1½ cups water

6 cups finely shredded cabbage

⅓ cup pickled ginger, plus more for serving

2 tablespoons sesame oil

2 green onions, sliced thinly

1 tablespoon sesame seeds, toasted

DIPPING SAUCE

¼ cup light soy sauce

1 tablespoon rice wine vinegar

2 teaspoons sesame oil

1 Whisk flour, cornstarch, eggs, and the water in a large bowl until smooth and combined; let stand for 15 minutes.

2 Meanwhile, preheat oven to 250°F. Line a baking sheet with parchment paper.

3 Meanwhile, make Dipping Sauce.

4 Add cabbage and ginger to the batter; stir to combine.

5 Heat 2 teaspoons of the oil in a large frying pan over medium heat. Spoon one quarter of the batter mixture into pan, flattening to form a 1-inch-thick pancake; cook pancake for 4 minutes on each side or until golden and cooked through. Transfer to baking sheet; keep warm in oven. Repeat process with remaining batter to make four pancakes in total.

6 Top pancakes with green onions, extra pickled ginger, and sesame seeds; serve with dipping sauce.

dipping sauce Combine ingredients in a small bowl.

serving suggestion Traditional condiments served with okonomiyaki are Japanese mayonnaise and spicy barbecue sauce (as pictured).

Everyday
VEGETARIAN

For the vegetarian who is happy to eat eggs and dairy foods. These recipes contain no meat or seafood.

Zucchini "spaghetti" WITH TOMATO & FETA

PREP + COOK TIME 55 MINUTES SERVES 4

Spaghetti-like strands are created from zucchini in this recipe instead of any actual pasta, which also makes this dish a great gluten-free option.

1 pound vine-ripened cherry tomatoes

6 tablespoons olive oil

4 tablespoons fresh oregano leaves, plus 2 tablespoons finely chopped fresh oregano

6-ounce piece feta, sliced lengthwise into 4 pieces

¼ teaspoon red pepper flakes

5 small zucchini

3 cloves garlic, sliced thinly

2 teaspoons finely grated lemon zest

¼ cup lemon juice

1 cup small fresh basil leaves

2 tablespoons coarsely grated parmesan

1 Preheat oven to 400°F. Line two baking sheets with parchment paper.

2 Place tomatoes on one baking sheet; drizzle with 1 tablespoon of the oil. Sprinkle with 2 tablespoons of the oregano leaves; season. Bake for 20 minutes or until golden and blistered.

3 Meanwhile, place feta slices on second baking sheet; drizzle with 1 more tablespoon of the oil. Sprinkle with pepper flakes and 1 more tablespoon of the oregano. Bake for 12 minutes or until golden.

4 Using a julienne peeler or spiralizer (see tips), cut zucchini into "spaghetti"; place in a large bowl.

5 Heat 2 more tablespoons oil in a small frying pan over medium heat; cook garlic for 2 minutes or until lightly golden. Stir in zest, juice, remaining 2 tablespoons oil and chopped oregano.

6 Add garlic mixture and roasted tomatoes (and any juices) to zucchini with basil and remaining 1 tablespoon oregano leaves; toss to combine. Season to taste. Serve 'spaghetti' topped with crumbled feta and parmesan.

tips To create the long pasta-like strands, you will need a few special tools: a julienne peeler (which looks like a wide bladed vegetable peeler with a serrated rather than straight blade), or a spiralizer, a hand-cranked machine designed to cut vegetables into noodles or ribbons. Both items are available from kitchenware shops.

Miso broth with tamari
SQUASH & NOODLES

PREP + COOK TIME 55 MINUTES   SERVES 4

⅓ cup red miso paste

¼ cup tamari

1 tablespoon olive oil

1¼ pounds butternut squash,
cut into 1-inch thick wedges

6 cups water

1½-ounce piece fresh ginger, cut into matchsticks

4 ounces dried soba noodles

½ pound gai lan (chinese broccoli), trimmed

¼ cup shredded dried seaweed (nori)

2 green onions, sliced thinly

2 tablespoons toasted sesame seeds

1 Preheat oven to 400°F. Line a baking sheet with parchment paper.

2 Whisk 1 tablespoon miso, 2 tablespoons tamari, and oil in a large bowl. Add squash; toss to coat. Place squash, in a single layer, on baking sheet. Roast for 40 minutes or until golden and tender.

3 Meanwhile, bring the water, ginger, and remaining miso to a boil in a large saucepan. Add noodles and gai lan; return to a boil. Reduce heat; simmer, for 2 minutes or until noodles are tender. Stir in remaining tamari; season to taste.

4 Divide squash and broth into bowls; sprinkle with seaweed, green onions, and seeds.

tip Just before serving, you could sprinkle this dish with a little shichimi togarashi—a Japanese spice powder (literally meaning "seven flavor chile pepper"). In addition to the chiles, other ingredients can include: sichuan pepper, dried citrus peel, sesame seeds, poppy seeds, hemp seeds, ginger, garlic, shiso, and nori. It is readily available from Asian supermarkets. If unavailable you can use red pepper flakes.

Asian noodle soup IN A JAR

PREP + COOK TIME 20 MINUTES SERVES 4

You will need four 2-cup heatproof jars with fitted lids for this recipe.

4 hard-boiled eggs, halved

1 tablespoon vegetarian tom yum paste

2 ounces dried rice vermicelli noodles

8 oyster mushrooms, torn

4 x 2-inch-long strips thinly sliced fresh ginger

4 fresh kaffir lime leaves, torn

8 cherry tomatoes, halved

⅓ cup bean sprouts

1 fresh long red chile, sliced thinly

1 lime, quartered

6 cups boiling water

¼ cup fresh cilantro leaves

1 Divide eggs, paste, noodles, mushrooms, ginger, lime leaves, tomatoes, sprouts, and chile among four 2-cup heatproof jars. Squeeze a lime quarter over ingredients in each jar; add lime to jars.

2 Pour 1½ cups of the boiling water into each jar; let stand, uncovered, for 6 minutes or until noodles are tender. Stir ingredients together. Serve topped with cilantro.

tips This recipe is perfect to take to work. Add more or less tom yum paste to taste. You can use boiling vegetable stock instead of boiling water for extra flavor.

Pasta with
RADISHES & THEIR TOPS

PREP + COOK TIME 20 MINUTES **SERVES** 4

This dish, which utilizes both the radish bulbs and tops, embodies the sustainability concept of root to leaf eating, where nothing goes to waste.

¼ cup currants

1½ tablespoons red wine vinegar

2 pounds baby red radishes, halved, leaves reserved

12 ounces dried spelt or whole-grain penne pasta

⅓ cup extra-virgin olive oil

1 clove garlic, crushed

⅓ cup toasted pine nuts

¼ cup fresh sage leaves

½ cup shaved pecorino cheese

1 Combine currants and vinegar in a small bowl; let stand for 15 minutes.

2 Meanwhile, coarsely chop reserved radish leaves.

3 Cook pasta in a large saucepan of boiling salted water until almost tender. Drain, reserving 1 cup cooking liquid.

4 Meanwhile, heat oil in a large frying pan over high heat; cook radishes, stirring occasionally, for 3 minutes or until browned. Add currant mixture, radish leaves, garlic, pine nuts, and sage; cook, stirring, for 1 minute or until fragrant and leaves are wilted. Season.

5 Add pasta to the frying pan with half the cheese, the remaining oil and enough of the reserved cooking liquid to coat; season to taste. Serve topped with remaining cheese.

tip Use the freshest, best radishes you can buy. The radishes should be firm, and the leaves crisp and bright green. We used 16 radishes and about 2½ cups of radish leaves in this recipe.

Sri Lankan
POTATO & PEA CURRY

PREP + COOK TIME 45 MINUTES   SERVES 4

4 medium potatoes, chopped coarsely

¼ cup ghee

1 medium yellow onion, sliced thinly

4 cloves garlic, chopped finely

2½ tablespoons finely chopped fresh ginger

2 sprigs fresh curry leaves

1 tablespoon curry powder

1½ teaspoons brown mustard seeds

½ teaspoon ground turmeric

2 fresh long green chiles, sliced thinly

1 can (15 oz) chickpeas (garbanzo beans), drained, rinsed

1 cup frozen peas

½ cup water

½ teaspoon finely grated lime zest

1 tablespoon lime juice

4 eggs

2 green onions, sliced thinly

1 cup fresh cilantro leaves

1 Place potatoes in a large saucepan with enough cold water to just cover; bring to a boil. Boil over medium heat for 15 minutes or until tender; drain.

2 Heat 2 tablespoons of the ghee in a large frying pan over medium heat; cook onion, stirring, for 5 minutes or until softened. Add garlic, ginger, curry leaves, curry powder, seeds, turmeric, and half the chiles; cook, stirring, for 1 minute or until fragrant.

3 Add potatoes, chickpeas, peas and the water; bring to a boil. Reduce heat; simmer, for 3 minutes or until peas are tender. Stir in zest and juice; season to taste.

4 Heat remaining ghee in a large frying pan over medium-high heat; fry eggs for 2 minutes or until the whites are set.

5 Serve potato curry topped with fried egg, green onions, cilantro, and remaining chile.

tip We used Yukon gold or red creamer potatoes.

Green goodness
IN A BOWL

PREP + COOK TIME 20 MINUTES   SERVES 4

¼ pound snow peas, trimmed

⅓ pound green beans, trimmed,
halved lengthwise

⅓ pound broccolini, halved on the diagonal

2 teaspoons olive oil

1 pound packaged brown microwave rice

3 tablespoons pepitas (pumpkin seeds), toasted

1 medium avocado, sliced thinly

AVOCADO YOGURT DRESSING

1 medium avocado, chopped coarsely

¾ cup Greek-style yogurt

¼ cup fresh basil leaves

2 tablespoons lime juice

1 small clove garlic, chopped finely

1 tablespoon olive oil

1 tablespoon water

1 Make Avocado Yogurt Dressing.

2 Boil, steam, or microwave peas, beans, and broccolini, separately, until tender; drain. Place peas, beans and broccolini in a large bowl with oil; toss to combine. Cover to keep warm.

3 Heat rice following instructions on package. Coarsely chop 2 tablespoons of the toasted pepitas and combine with rice in a medium bowl; season to taste.

4 Serve rice topped with three-quarters of the dressing, then vegetables, avocado, remaining dressing, and remaining 1 tablespoon toasted pepitas.

avocado yogurt dressing Blend or process ingredients until smooth and combined; season to taste.

tip For a spicy version, add 2 teaspoons chopped pickled jalapeños to the dressing.

Lentil sausage rolls
WITH TOMATO SUMAC SALAD

PREP + COOK TIME 45 MINUTES SERVES 4

2 cans (15 oz each) lentils, drained, rinsed

1 small yellow onion, grated finely

2 cloves garlic, crushed

⅓ cup coarsely chopped, toasted pistachios

1 teaspoon sweet paprika

1 teaspoon ground cumin

¼ teaspoon ground cinnamon

¼ teaspoon red pepper flakes

1 egg, beaten lightly

10 sheets filo pastry

cooking oil spray

½ teaspoon sumac

⅔ cup Greek-style yogurt

TOMATO SUMAC SALAD

6 ounces mixed baby tomatoes, chopped

½ small red onion, sliced thinly

1 tablespoon thinly sliced preserved-lemon rind

3 ounces mesclun

½ cup fresh flat-leaf parsley leaves

1½ tablespoons olive oil

1½ tablespoons lemon juice

½ teaspoon sumac

1 Preheat oven to 400°F. Line a baking sheet with parchment paper.

2 Place lentils in a large bowl; mash lightly. Add onion, garlic, pistachios, paprika, cumin, cinnamon, pepper flakes, and egg; stir to combine. Season.

3 Layer five sheets of filo, spraying each sheet with oil (cover remaining filo sheets with a clean, damp kitchen towel). Place half the lentil mixture along one long side of filo; roll to enclose filling. Cut into four even lengths. Place on baking sheet; spray with oil. Repeat with remaining filo, oil spray, and lentil mixture to make 8 rolls in total.

4 Sprinkle rolls with sumac; bake for 30 minutes or until golden and crisp.

5 Meanwhile, make Tomato Sumac Salad.

6 Serve lentil rolls with salad and yogurt.

tomato sumac salad Place ingredients in a large bowl; toss to combine.

Cooking by the seasons means...

You will have flavorful produce that you'll be even more inspired to eat.

Just think of the difference between a firm tomato and a warm sun-ripened one.

It also means that you will be paying less for fruit and veg. So stock up,

make extra, and freeze in order to enjoy into the next season.

Roasted VEGGIES

Vegetables you might not have thought to roast:

FENNEL Quarter baby fennel or slice large bulbs, drizzle with oil, and roast until caramelized.

CORN Roast halved cobs in a pan at a high temperature for 20 minutes; serve with miso butter.

CAULIFLOWER Combine florets with a little honey, turmeric, and olive oil, and roast until golden and tender. Toss with currants soaked in vinegar, dukkah, and herbs.

GLOBE ARTICHOKE Place cooked artichoke hearts in a buttered shallow flameproof dish; roast until crisp.

CELERY ROOT Roast as you would squash, for about 1 hour at 400°F until it is a golden brown color.

LEFTOVER RICE CAN BE USED FOR...

BINDING VEGETABLE PATTIES AND FRITTATAS TOGETHER; AS A FILLING IN SPANAKOPITA (SEE PAGE 144); OR PROCESS WITH SOME SEEDS AND A LITTLE EGG TO MAKE A 'PASTRY' CRUST, BAKE IN A 400°F OVEN UNTIL CRISP, THEN TOP WITH SLICED HEIRLOOM TOMATOES AND TORN BASIL.

Hardy herbs

Leftover woody herbs, like thyme and rosemary, can be hung up to dry, or strip the leaves from the stems and pop them into ice-cube trays; top up with olive oil and freeze for up to 1 month. Use straight from the freezer when cooking.

TURN A COUPLE OF ZUCCHINI INTO...

Fritters Coarsely grate zucchini, squeeze out excess moisture, and combine with an egg, mint, ½ cup crumbled feta, and a little flour to bind. Fry patties in olive oil.

Chargrilled salad Chargrill zucchini slices with wedges of red onion, then toss with kalamata olives, basil, and torn buffalo mozzarella.

NUT *Milks*

When you make the nut milks on page 170, you will be left with the dry, but still edible, nut meal. This mixture can be frozen, then used in one of the following ways:

Combine with *curry pastes*

Thicken *soups, stew,* or *curries*

Sprinkle on *muesli* or add to *smoothies* to boost your fiber intake

As a binder in *vegetable patties* and other soft mixtures instead of bread crumbs

MONEY $AVER
KEEPING THE PEEL ON YOUR VEG SAVES TIME AND NUTRIENTS

WASTE NOT *want not*

VEGETABLES WITH EDIBLE TOPS:

RADISHES	BEET	TURNIPS	FENNEL	KOHLRABI
Shallow-fry the peppery tops in a little olive oil (see also page 157).	Add the small earthy leaves to salads; fry the bigger leaves with their finely chopped stems.	Shallow-fry the mustardy tasting leaves in a little olive oil, season to taste; toss with lemon juice.	Finely chop the feathery fronds or pick into small sprigs; use as you would dill, for a gentle anise taste.	Stir-fry these cabbage-tasting leaves and stems in a little sesame or olive oil, or a combination of both.

Breaded zucchini & SLAW WRAPS

PREP + COOK TIME 40 MINUTES   SERVES 4

2 medium zucchini, sliced thinly, lengthwise

2 eggs, beaten lightly

1⅓ cups panko (japanese) bread crumbs

¼ cup olive oil

1 small head lettuce, leaves separated

4 x 8-inch whole-grain wraps

WHITE BARBECUE SAUCE

¼ teaspoon garlic powder

¼ teaspoon cayenne pepper

2 teaspoons horseradish cream

⅓ cup mayonnaise

1 tablespoon lemon juice

1 tablespoon water

SLAW

1 cup finely shredded red cabbage

½ small white onion, sliced thinly

1 medium carrot, grated coarsely

⅔ cup crunchy sprouts

1 Make White Barbecue Sauce, then the Slaw.

2 Dip zucchini in egg, then coat in bread crumbs, pressing lightly to secure.

3 Heat half the oil in a large frying pan over medium-high heat; cook half the zucchini for 3 minutes or until both sides are golden and tender. Repeat with remaining oil and zucchini.

4 Place lettuce along center of each wrap; top evenly with Slaw, zucchini, and remaining White Barbecue Sauce. Roll to enclose filling.

white barbecue sauce Stir ingredients in a small bowl.

slaw Place cabbage, onion, carrot, sprouts, and half the White Barbecue Sauce in a medium bowl; toss to combine. Season to taste.

Potato, bell pepper & SPINACH FRITTATA

PREP + COOK TIME 40 MINUTES SERVES 4

1 pound baby new potatoes

8 eggs

⅔ cup milk

1 tablespoon olive oil

3 ounces baby spinach leaves

1 cup chargrilled red bell pepper, drained, chopped coarsely

3 ounces soft goat cheese, crumbled

1 tablespoon lemon zest strips (see tip)

OLIVE SALSA

¼ cup pitted kalamata olives, chopped

¼ cup pitted green sicilian olives, chopped

¼ cup pitted green olives, chopped

½ small red onion, chopped finely

¼ cup chopped fresh flat-leaf parsley

pinch red pepper flakes

1 tablespoon olive oil

2 teaspoons lemon juice

1 Place potatoes in a medium saucepan with enough cold water to just cover. Boil over medium heat for 15 minutes or until potatoes are tender; drain. Cut into 1-inch pieces.

2 Meanwhile, make Olive Salsa.

3 Whisk eggs and milk in a medium bowl; season.

4 Preheat broiler.

5 Heat oil in a heavy-bottomed frying pan over medium-high heat; cook spinach until wilted. Add potatoes and bell pepper; cook, stirring, for 1 minute. Add egg mixture. Reduce heat to medium; cook for 7 minutes or until egg is almost set. Top with cheese. Place under broiler for 3 minutes or until golden and set.

6 Serve frittata with salsa; sprinkle with lemon rind.

olive salsa Combine ingredients in a small bowl.

tip If you have one, use a zester to create the strips of lemon zest. If you don't have one, peel two long, wide strips of zest from the lemon, without the white pith, then cut them lengthwise into thin strips.

NUT MILK

PREP TIME 10 MINUTES (+ **STANDING**)
MAKES 2 CUPS

You can make nut milks with most nuts: hazelnuts, almonds, cashews, pecans. If you want to sweeten the milk, add pure maple syrup, honey, or puréed dates.

Place 1 cup skinless hazelnuts in a large bowl; cover with cold water. Stand, covered, for 4 hours or overnight. Drain; rinse under cold water. Drain. Process nuts with 2 cups water until smooth. Pour mixture through a strainer lined with cheesecloth into a large bowl. Keep any blended nuts left behind for another use (see tips opposite).

SPICED NUT MILK

VANILLA NUT MILK

TIPS

Using skinless or blanched nuts will create a whiter colored milk.

Dry out the strained, blended nuts on baking sheet in a 300°F oven. Sprinkle on your breakfast cereal or add to curries and pastes.

Using a high-powered blender such as a Vitamix will create a smoother textured milk.

SPICED NUT MILK

Make nut milk on opposite page using 1 cup pecans. Stir in cinnamon sticks, star anise, and saffron threads.

VANILLA NUT MILK

Make nut milk on opposite page using ½ cup almonds and ½ cup cashews. Split a vanilla bean lengthwise, scrape the seeds into the milk; stir to combine.

Cheese & SWISS CHARD BOREK

PREP + COOK TIME 1 HOUR 20 MINUTES SERVES 6

6 large stalks swiss chard

cooking oil spray

5 eggs

1 pound cottage cheese

6 ounces feta, crumbled

1 cup sour cream

¾ cup soda water

8 ounces filo pastry

1 teaspoon poppy seeds

1 tablespoon sunflower seeds

1 tablespoon pepitas (pumpkin seeds)

1 Preheat oven to 325°F. Grease an 8¾-inch x 12¾-inch x 2½-inch rectangular ovenproof dish.

2 Trim 1½ inches from swiss chard stems; separate leaves and stems. Finely shred leaves; finely chop stems. You will need 4 cups shredded leaves and 1½ cups finely chopped stems.

3 Lightly spray a large frying pan over high heat; cook chard leaves and stems for 2 minutes or until wilted and tender. When cool enough to handle, squeeze excess water from chard; set aside to cool.

4 Whisk 4 of the eggs in a large bowl until combined. Add cottage cheese, feta, sour cream, soda water, and chard; stir to combine, season.

5 Layer five sheets of pastry, spraying each sheet with oil; place on base of dish. Pour 1 cup of cheese mixture on pastry.

6 Layer two sheets of pastry, spraying each sheet with oil; place on cheese mixture. Pour 1 cup of cheese mixture on pastry. Repeat layering with two more sheets of pastry and remaining cheese mixture. Layer five sheets of pastry, spraying each sheet with oil; place on cheese mixture.

7 Whisk remaining egg in a small bowl. Brush egg over top of pie; sprinkle with seeds. Bake pie for 50 minutes or until golden and cooked through.

tip When you're not working with filo pastry, keep it covered with a clean, damp kitchen towel. This will help keep it from drying out.

Roasted cauliflower & BRUSSELS SPROUTS

PREP + COOK TIME 45 MINUTES   SERVES 4

⅓ cup olive oil

1½ teaspoons ground cumin

1 teaspoon nigella seeds

2 teaspoons toasted sesame seeds

2 tablespoons honey

1 small cauliflower, trimmed, cut into florets

1 pound brussels sprouts

¼ cup pine nuts

2 tablespoons fresh cilantro leaves

2 tablespoons fresh mint leaves

TAHINI DRESSING

½ cup tahini

⅓ cup lemon juice

1 clove garlic, crushed

¼ cup cold water

2 tablespoons finely chopped fresh cilantro

2 tablespoons finely chopped fresh mint

1 Preheat oven to 425°F. Line a baking sheet with parchment paper.
2 Combine oil, cumin, seeds, and honey in a large bowl; season. Add cauliflower and sprouts; toss to combine. Place vegetable mixture on baking sheet.
3 Bake for 15 minutes or until vegetables are almost tender. Add nuts to baking sheet; bake for a further 5 minutes or until nuts are golden and vegetables are tender.
4 Meanwhile, make Tahini Dressing.
5 Serve vegetables topped with the herbs and drizzled with tahini dressing.

tahini dressing Combine ingredients a small bowl; season to taste.

tips Nigella seeds, also known as kolonji, are the seeds sprinkled on Turkish bread. They are available at many grocery stores and online; you can substitute cumin seeds. Before using tahini always stir the oil that sits on top of the paste back into it and ensure that any liquid that is added to thin tahini is cold and not hot, otherwise it will thicken the tahini instead.

serving suggestion Serve with warmed flatbread.

Tomato, tofu & CHILE PILAF

PREP + COOK TIME 35 MINUTES SERVES 6

¼ cup butter

2 small red onions, sliced thinly

11 ounces thai-flavored marinated tofu, cut into 1-inch pieces (see tip)

1½ cups jasmine rice

2 teaspoons finely grated ginger

1 fresh long red chile, seeded, chopped finely

2 tablespoons thai red curry paste

1 can (14.5 oz) chopped tomatoes

1½ cups boiling water

⅓ pound snow peas, trimmed

¼ cup toasted peanuts, chopped coarsely

2 green onions, sliced thinly

¼ cup fresh cilantro sprigs

1 lime, cut into wedges

1 Heat butter in a 10½-inch frying pan over medium heat; cook red onion, and tofu, stirring occasionally, for 5 minutes or until onions soften and tofu browns slightly.
2 Meanwhile, place rice in a sieve; rinse under cold running water until water runs clear. Set aside.
3 Add ginger, chile, and curry paste to pan; increase heat to high. Stir for 3 minutes or until mixture starts to stick a little and caramelize. Stir in rinsed rice until well coated. Add tomatoes and the water; season generously with salt.
4 Bring to a boil, cover with a lid; reduce heat to low, cook for 15 minutes or until liquid is absorbed. Remove pan from heat; place snow peas on rice. Cover pan; let stand, for 5 minutes (the residual heat will finish cooking the snow peas and rice).
5 Serve pilaf topped with peanuts, green onions, cilantro, and lime wedges.

tip Use another flavored tofu or even plain tofu instead, **if** you prefer.

Swiss chard omelet
WITH BELL PEPPER SALAD

PREP + COOK TIME 35 MINUTES **SERVES** 4

8 ounces chargrilled red bell pepper, drained, sliced thickly

1 tablespoon fresh thyme leaves

3 cloves garlic, crushed

1 tablespoon balsamic vinegar

1 tablespoon olive oil

6 medium stalks swiss chard

10 free-range eggs

¼ cup milk

3 cups firmly packed snow pea tendrils

½ cup shaved pecorino cheese

1 Combine bell pepper, thyme, 1 clove of the crushed garlic, vinegar, and oil in a large bowl; let stand for 15 minutes.

2 Meanwhile, cut stems from swiss chard (save for another use if you like); shred leaves. Whisk eggs, milk, shredded chard, and remaining 2 cloves crushed garlic in a large bowl; season.

3 Heat a small non-stick frying pan over medium heat. Pour one-quarter of the egg mixture into pan; tilt pan to cover base with egg mixture. Cook over medium heat for 3 minutes or until omelet is just set. Carefully slide omelet onto plate; cover to keep warm. Repeat with remaining egg mixture to make 4 omelets in total.

4 Add snow pea tendrils and pecorino to bell pepper mixture; toss to combine.

5 Serve omelets topped with bell pepper salad.

Roasted vegetables with
BASIL & FETA POLENTA

PREP + COOK TIME 50 MINUTES SERVES 6

1 pound squash, chopped coarsely

2 large zucchini, chopped coarsely

2 medium red onions, quartered

2 large red bell peppers, chopped coarsely

1 tablespoon cumin seeds

2 teaspoons ground coriander

½ teaspoon red pepper flakes

2 cloves garlic, crushed

¼ cup olive oil

2 tablespoons red wine vinegar

6 cups vegetable stock (see page 40)

1½ cups polenta

6 ounces feta, crumbled

½ cup torn fresh basil

⅓ cup coarsely chopped toasted hazelnuts

1 Preheat oven to 425°F. Line two large baking sheets with parchment paper.

2 Combine squash, zucchini, onions, bell peppers, cumin, coriander, pepper flakes, garlic, and oil in a large bowl; season. Place vegetables on baking sheets; roast for 30 minutes or until golden and tender. Drizzle with vinegar.

3 Meanwhile, bring stock to a boil in a large saucepan. Gradually add polenta, whisking continuously. Reduce heat; simmer, stirring, for 10 minutes or until polenta thickens. Stir in 4 ounces of the feta and ⅓ cup of the basil.

4 Serve polenta immediately, topped with vegetables, hazelnuts, remaining feta, and remaining basil.

Broccoli, mustard & CHEDDAR HAND PIES

PREP + COOK TIME 30 MINUTES   SERVES 6

6 sheets puff pastry

½ cup honey mustard

½ pound broccoli, chopped finely

1½ cups grated cheddar

1½ cups grated mozzarella

1 egg, beaten lightly

3 teaspoons toasted sesame seeds

1 Preheat oven to 400°F. Line two baking sheets with parchment paper.

2 Using a plate as a guide, cut six 8¾-inch rounds from the pastry. Spread pastry with mustard, leaving a ½-inch border around the edge.

3 Combine broccoli, cheddar and mozzarella in a large bowl; season. Place one-sixth of the broccoli mixture in the center of a pastry round; fold over to enclose filling, crimping the edge to seal. Repeat with remaining broccoli mixture and pastry rounds.

4 Place pies on baking sheets. Brush with egg and sprinkle with seeds; cut four slashes on each pie.

5 Bake pies for 25 minutes or until golden and puffed.

tip Pies can be made the day before up to the end of step 3; store, covered, in the fridge.

serving suggestion Serve with a simple green salad.

Carrot & chickpea salad
WITH HARISSA GOAT'S CHEESE

PREP + COOK TIME 15 MINUTES **SERVES** 4

2 tablespoons garlic oil

2 tablespoons lemon juice

2 teaspoons honey

¾ pound carrots, shredded (see tips)

1 large can (28 oz) chickpeas (garbanzo beans), drained, rinsed

1 small red onion, sliced thinly

½ cup golden raisins

½ cup sliced almonds, toasted

1 cup fresh mint leaves

6 ounces goat's cheese

3 teaspoons harissa paste

2 whole-grain lebanese breads, warmed

1 medium lemon, cut into wedges

1 Combine oil, juice, and honey in a large bowl. Add carrots, chickpeas, red onion, sultanas, almonds, and mint; toss to combine. Season to taste.

2 Combine curd and harissa in a small bowl.

3 Serve salad topped with curd mixture. Serve with bread and lemon wedges.

tips We used a julienne peeler to easily shred the carrot into long thin strips. They are available from kitchenware shops and most supermarkets. Harissa is a hot paste; there are many different brands available, and the strengths vary enormously. If you have a low heat-level tolerance, you may find this, and any other recipe containing harissa, too hot to tolerate, even if you reduce the amount.

Green quinoa
WITH SESAME EGGS

PREP + COOK TIME 25 MINUTES SERVES 2

1 cup vegetable stock

½ cup white quinoa, rinsed

4 eggs, at room temperature

2 teaspoons coconut oil

1 small clove garlic, crushed

1 fresh small red chile, sliced thinly

2 cups thinly sliced kale (see tips)

2 cups firmly packed, thinly sliced swiss chard
(see tips)

1 tablespoon lemon juice

¼ cup finely chopped fresh flat-leaf parsley

1 tablespoon white sesame seeds

1 tablespoon black sesame seeds

1 teaspoon flaky sea salt

1 Place stock and quinoa in a medium saucepan; bring to a boil. Reduce heat to low-medium; simmer gently for 15 minutes or until most of the stock is absorbed. Remove from heat; cover, let stand 5 minutes.
2 Meanwhile, cook eggs in a small saucepan of boiling water for 5 minutes. Remove immediately from boiling water; cool under running cold water for 30 seconds.
3 Heat coconut oil in a medium saucepan over medium heat. Add garlic and chile; cook ,stirring, for 2 minutes or until fragrant. Add kale and swiss chard; stir until wilted. Add cooked quinoa and juice; season to taste.
4 Combine parsley, both sesame seeds, and salt in a small bowl. Peel eggs; roll in parsley mixture.
5 Serve quinoa topped with eggs.

tips You will need to buy 1 bunch kale and 1 bunch swiss chard. Leftover greens can be wilted in a little olive oil or chopped and added to soups.

Chickpea SHAKSHUKA

PREP + COOK TIME 30 MINUTES SERVES 4

1 teaspoon caraway seeds

1 teaspoon cumin seeds

1 teaspoon smoked paprika

2 tablespoons olive oil

2 cloves garlic, crushed

1 fresh long red chile, chopped finely

1 large yellow onion, chopped coarsely

1 large red bell pepper, chopped coarsely

1 can (15 oz) chickpeas (garbanzo beans), drained, rinsed

1 can (14.5 oz) diced tomatoes

1 cup water

2 teaspoons harissa

2 teaspoons superfine sugar

4 eggs

¼ cup fresh cilantro leaves

1 Heat a large, deep ovenproof frying pan over medium heat; cook seeds and paprika, stirring, for 1 minute or until fragrant. Add oil, garlic, and chile; cook for 1 minute or until fragrant.

2 Add onion and bell pepper; cook, stirring, for 8 minutes or until onion is softened. Add chickpeas, tomatoes, the water, harissa, and sugar; bring to a boil. Reduce heat; simmer, for 5 minutes or until vegetables are tender and liquid has thickened slightly.

3 Using a spoon, make four shallow indents in the tomato mixture. Crack 1 egg into each hole. Cook, covered, on low heat, for 5 minutes or until whites are set and yolks still remain runny, or until cooked to your liking. Serve topped with cilantro.

tip Harissa is a hot paste; there are many different brands available, and the strengths vary enormously. If you have a low heat-level tolerance, you may find this, and any other recipe containing harissa, too hot to tolerate, even if you reduce the amount.

serving suggestion Serve with baked chia seed lavash and chile oil. Preheat oven to 425°F. Spray lavash with cooking oil and cut into quarters. Bake for 8 minutes or until golden and crisp.

Smoked tofu salad
WITH PEANUT DRESSING

PREP + COOK TIME 45 MINUTES   SERVES 4

4 eggs

¼ cup water

1 tablespoon fried shallots

1 teaspoon tamari

1 tablespoon sesame oil

11 ounces smoked tofu, cut into ½-inch pieces

1 medium avocado, sliced thinly

½ pound cherry tomatoes, halved

1½ cups bean sprouts

½ cup fresh cilantro leaves

½ cup fresh mint leaves

2½ ounces baby salad leaves

2 tablespoons black sesame seeds

PEANUT DRESSING

⅓ cup toasted peanuts, chopped coarsely

1 green onion, sliced thinly

1 fresh long red chile, sliced thinly

1 teaspoon finely grated fresh ginger

1 clove garlic, crushed

1½ tablespoons grated palm sugar

2 tablespoons sesame oil

2 tablespoons tamari

¼ cup rice vinegar

1½ tablespoons lime juice

1 Make Peanut Dressing.

2 Whisk eggs, the water, shallots, and tamari in a large bowl; season.

3 Heat oil in a wok over medium heat. Pour half the egg mixture into wok; cook, tilting wok, until almost set. Remove omelet from wok. Repeat with remaining egg mixture. Roll omelets tightly, then slice thinly; reserve.

4 Place tofu in a large bowl with remaining ingredients and Peanut Dressing; toss to combine.

5 Serve tofu salad topped with reserved omelet.

peanut dressing Whisk ingredients in a medium bowl until combined.

tips Smoked tofu can be found at health food stores, you can also use regular firm tofu instead for this recipe.
To keep mung bean sprouts crisp and crunchy, store them in cold water in the fridge for up to 3 days.

Carrot, feta & QUINOA TARTS

PREP + COOK TIME 45 MINUTES SERVES 8

¾ pound baby carrots, unpeeled

½ cup fresh ricotta

3 ounces feta, crumbled

1 clove garlic, crushed

1 egg

¼ teaspoon fennel seeds

¼ teaspoon cumin seeds

¼ cup finely grated parmesan

2 tablespoons extra-virgin olive oil

1 cup Greek-style yogurt

½ cup snow pea tendrils

QUINOA DOUGH

1⅔ cups all-purpose flour

¼ cup red quinoa

½ teaspoon active dried yeast

1 teaspoon flaked sea salt

⅓ cup extra-virgin olive oil

⅔ cup hot water

1 Make Quinoa Dough.

2 Preheat oven to 425°F.

3 Trim carrot tops, leaving ¾-inch stem attached; reserve a small handful of the tops. Wash carrots and tops. Finely chop carrot tops; you'll need 2 tablespoons. Combine chopped carrot tops with ricotta, feta, garlic, and egg in a medium bowl. Season.

4 Divide the dough in half. Roll out one half of the dough on a piece of lightly floured parchment paper into a 4½-inch x 16-inch oval. Lift paper and dough onto a large baking sheet. Repeat with remaining pastry and a second baking sheet.

5 Spread each oval with half the cheese mixture; top with carrots. Sprinkle with seeds and parmesan; drizzle with oil; season.

6 Bake tarts for 25 minutes or until pastry is golden and cooked through. Serve tart slices topped with spoonfuls of yogurt and snow pea tendrils.

quinoa dough Place ingredients, except the hot water, in a food processor; pulse for a few seconds until combined. With motor running, add the water; process for 3 minutes until well combined. Form dough into a ball; wrap in plastic wrap. Set aside.

Everyday
VEGAN

For the vegetarian who only eats plant-based foods. These recipes contain no meat, no seafood, no dairy, and no eggs.

Eggplant
MA PO TOFU

PREP + COOK TIME 35 MINUTES   SERVES 4

6 baby eggplants, halved lengthwise, scored

2 tablespoons vegetable oil

2 cloves garlic, sliced thinly

¾-ounce piece fresh ginger, cut into matchsticks

4 green onions, sliced thinly

3 shiitake mushrooms, sliced thinly

1½ tablespoons chili sauce

½ cup vegetable stock (see page 40)

1 tablespoon soy sauce

1¼ pounds silken tofu, cut into 2-inch pieces

1 teaspoon cornstarch

2 tablespoons water

2 teaspoons toasted sichuan pepper, ground

2 tablespoons coarsely chopped fresh garlic chives

1 Steam eggplant, covered, over a large wok of simmering water for 20 minutes or until tender.

2 Meanwhile, heat oil in a large wok over high heat; stir-fry garlic, ginger, and half the green onion, for 30 seconds or until fragrant. Add mushrooms and chili bean sauce; stir-fry for 1 minute. Add stock and soy sauce; bring to a boil. Add tofu; reduce heat, simmer, for 3 minutes or until warmed through.

3 Combine cornstarch with the water in a small bowl; add to tofu mixture. Return to a boil; boil until mixture thickens. Remove from heat. Stir in ground pepper and three-quarters of the chives.

4 Serve eggplant topped with tofu mixture, and sprinkled with remaining chives and remaining green onion.

Green dumplings with
SOY CHILE DIPPING SAUCE

PREP + COOK TIME 45 MINUTES   SERVES 4

½ pound spinach, trimmed

¼ pound gai lan (chinese broccoli) leaves

1 cup fresh finely chopped garlic chives

2 tablespoons soy sauce

2 cloves garlic, grated finely

1½ tablespoons finely grated fresh ginger

2 teaspoons sesame oil

½ pound round gow gee wrappers

SOY CHILI DIPPING SAUCE

¼ cup soy sauce

2 tablespoon chinese black vinegar

1 teaspoon superfine sugar

1 teaspoon sesame oil

1 teaspoon chili oil

1 green onion, sliced thinly

1 Boil, steam, or microwave spinach and gai lan until tender; drain. Rinse under cold water; drain. Squeeze out excess water; chop finely.

2 Combine spinach, gai lan, chives, sauce, garlic, ginger, and oil in a medium bowl.

3 Place 2 teaspoons of mixture in the center of a gow gee wrapper. Wet edge of wrapper with fingers; fold in half and press edges together to seal. Repeat with remaining wrappers and mixture.

4 Cook dumplings, in batches, in a large saucepan of boiling water, for 2 minutes, or until they float and are just tender. Drain.

5 Meanwhile, make Soy Chili Dipping sauce.

6 Serve dumplings with dipping sauce.

soy chili dipping sauce Combine ingredients in a small bowl.

tip To turn this recipe into a dumpling soup, serve dumplings in vegetable stock (see page 40).

Vietnamese coconut & TURMERIC PANCAKES

PREP + COOK TIME 25 MINUTES (+ STANDING)   SERVES 4

⅔ cup coconut milk

⅔ cup water

½ cup rice flour

1 teaspoon ground turmeric

¼ cup vegetable oil

1 package (8 oz) tempeh, cut into 8 slices

2 tablespoon hoisin sauce

8 butter (boston) lettuce leaves

2 persian cucumbers, cut into matchsticks

1 cup fresh mint leaves

1 cup fresh cilantro leaves

1 cup fresh thai basil leaves

1 cup bean sprouts

PICKLED CARROT

⅓ cup rice wine vinegar

2 teaspoons superfine sugar

2 medium carrots, cut into matchsticks (see tips)

1 fresh long red chile, sliced thinly

LEMON GARLIC DIPPING SAUCE

¼ cup lemon juice

2 teaspoons superfine sugar

2 teaspoons soy sauce

1 small clove garlic, chopped finely

1 Whisk coconut milk, the water, flour, and turmeric in a medium bowl until smooth and combined. Let stand for 1 hour.

2 Meanwhile, make Pickled Carrot, then Lemon Garlic Dipping sauce.

3 Heat 1 tablespoon oil in a large, non-stick frying pan over medium high heat; cook tempeh for 1 minute or until golden. Remove from pan.

4 Heat 2 teaspoons oil in a large nonstick frying pan over medium-high heat. Pour one-quarter of the batter into pan, tilt pan to cover base with batter; cook for 2 minutes or until pancake is just set. Carefully slide pancake onto plate; cover with foil to keep warm. Repeat with remaining batter to make 4 pancakes in total.

5 Spread pancakes with hoisin sauce; top with tempeh, lettuce, cucumber, Pickled Carrot, herbs, and sprouts. Serve with dipping sauce.

pickled carrot Whisk vinegar and sugar in a large bowl; add carrot and chile, then toss to combine. Let stand, stirring occasionally, for 15 minutes.

lemon garlic dipping sauce Whisk ingredients in a small bowl; season to taste.

tips We used a julienne peeler to easily cut the carrot into long thin strips. They are available from kitchenware shops and most major supermarkets.

Carrot & lentil soup
WITH CILANTRO PESTO

PREP + COOK TIME 50 MINUTES **SERVES** 4

2 tablespoons olive oil

1 large yellow onion, chopped coarsely

1½ pounds carrots, chopped coarsely

2 teaspoons ground cumin

2 teaspoons ground coriander

pinch red pepper flakes

1 cup red lentils

4 cups vegetable stock (see page 40)

1½ cups water

½ cup fresh cilantro leaves

CILANTRO PESTO

1 cup fresh cilantro leaves

1 small clove garlic, crushed

2 tablespoons toasted pistachios

¼ cup olive oil

1 tablespoon lemon juice

1 Heat oil in a large saucepan over medium heat; cook onion and carrot, covered, stirring occasionally, for 10 minutes or until softened. Add cumin, coriander, and pepper flakes; stir to coat. Add lentils and stock; bring to a boil. Reduce heat; simmer, covered, for 35 minutes or until lentils and carrots are soft.

2 Meanwhile, make Cilantro Pesto.

3 Blend or process soup until smooth. Return soup to pan with the water; bring to a boil. Season to taste. Serve soup drizzled with pesto, topped with cilantro leaves.

cilantro pesto Blend or process cilantro, garlic, and pistachios until finely chopped. With motor operating, add oil and juice in a thin, steady stream until combined. Season to taste.

tip Lentils will thicken on standing; if necessary add a little extra water or stock to thin the soup.

serving suggestion Serve with sourdough bread.

Roasted beet
& MILLET SALAD

PREP + COOK TIME 1 HOUR 20 MINUTES SERVES 4

2 pounds baby beets, unpeeled, trimmed

¼ cup olive oil

⅔ cup hulled millet (see tips)

2 cups water

1 medium fennel, sliced thinly

½ small red onion, sliced thinly

6 stalks rainbow chard, shredded finely

⅓ cup coarsely chopped, toasted
unsalted pistachios

2 tablespoons coarsely chopped fresh dill

¼ cup coarsely chopped fresh flat-leaf parsley

HARISSA DRESSING

¼ cup olive oil

1½ tablespoons sherry vinegar

3 teaspoons harissa

1 tablespoon lemon juice

1 Preheat oven to 400°F. Line a baking sheet with parchment paper.

2 Place beets on baking sheet; drizzle with a little of the oil. Roast for 50 minutes or until tender. Peel and discard skins; halve or quarter beets depending on size.

3 Meanwhile, place millet in a medium saucepan, cover with the water; bring to a boil, stirring occasionally. Reduce heat; simmer, for 15 minutes or until millet is almost tender. Drain. Return millet to pan with remaining oil; cook, stirring, over medium heat for 3 minutes or until millet is dry. Season to taste.

4 Meanwhile, make Harissa Dressing.

5 Place beet and millet in a large bowl with fennel, onion, chard, pistachios, herbs, and dressing; toss gently to combine.

harissa dressing Place ingredients in a screw-top jar; shake well. Season to taste.

tips Harissa is a hot chile paste; there are many different brands available on the market, and the strengths vary enormously. Harissa in a tube is generally much hotter than brands from a jar. Taste a little first before using. In ancient times millet was more widely consumed in Asia than rice is today. Like rice, it is gluten-free, making it suitable for those on low, or gluten-free diets. It is almost always sold in its whole-grain form in health food stores and so provides fiber, B-group vitamins, and plant proteins.

Sweet potato & "CHORIZO" TACOS

PREP + COOK TIME 40 MINUTES SERVES 4

2 small sweet potatoes, unpeeled

½ cup olive oil

6 green onions, chopped coarsely

1 teaspoon ground cumin

1 teaspoon ground coriander

2 cups coarsely chopped fresh cilantro leaves and stems

2 fresh jalapeño chiles, chopped coarsely

1½ teaspoons finely grated lime zest

2 tablespoons lime juice

⅓ cup water

1 jar (16 oz) sun-dried tomatoes in oil

¼ teaspoon garlic powder

¼ teaspoon onion powder

½ teaspoon smoked paprika

¼ cup toasted whole blanched almonds

¼ cup toasted walnuts

12 x 6¾-inch white corn tortillas, warmed

2 ounces baby arugula leaves

1 Boil, steam, or microwave sweet potatoes until tender; drain. When cool enough to handle, peel sweet potatoes; cut flesh into ¾-inch pieces.

2 Meanwhile, blend or process oil, onions, cumin, ground coriander, cilantro, chiles, zest, juice, and the water in a food processor until smooth. Transfer to a small bowl; stand until required.

3 Drain oil from tomatoes over a bowl; reserve. Coarsely chop tomatoes. Process tomatoes and 2 tablespoons of the reserved oil with garlic and onion powders, paprika, and nuts until coarsely chopped. Add 2 tablespoons of cilantro mixture; pulse until combined.

4 Transfer tomato mixture to a large frying pan, stir in sweet potato. Heat mixture over low heat for 5 minutes or until warmed through. Serve sweet potato mixture in tortillas with arugula and remaining cilantro mixture.

Vegetable
BEAN CURD ROLLS

PREP + COOK TIME 45 MINUTES SERVES 4

2 ounces dried rice vermicelli noodles

1 tablespoon sesame oil

⅓ pound shiitake mushrooms, sliced thinly

¼ pound enoki mushrooms, trimmed

3 cups finely shredded napa cabbage

⅓ pound green beans, sliced thinly

1 medium carrot, cut into matchsticks

1 cup mung bean sprouts

⅓ cup char siu sauce

2 tablespoons tamari or soy sauce

2 tablespoons toasted sesame seeds

4 bean curd sheets (see tips)

1 teaspoon cornstarch

1 Place noodles in a small heatproof bowl, cover with boiling water, and let stand until just tender; drain.
2 Heat oil in a wok over high heat; stir-fry mushrooms for 2 minutes or until golden and tender. Add napa cabbage, beans and carrot; stir-fry for 1 minute or until almost tender. Add sprouts, noodles, 2 tablespoons of the char siu sauce, half the tamari and half the sesame seeds; stir-fry for 30 seconds or until heated through. Drain, reserving cooking liquid.
3 Halve bean curd sheets. Top with ½ cup of the vegetable mixture. Fold sheet over filling, then fold in both sides. Continue rolling to enclose filling. Repeat with remaining vegetable mixture and sheets to make a total of eight rolls.
4 Steam rolls, covered, over a large wok of simmering water for 10 minutes or until bean curd is tender.
5 Meanwhile, whisk cornstarch and reserved cooking liquid in a small saucepan until combined. Stir in remaining char siu sauce, tamari, and seeds. Place pan over medium-high heat; cook, uncovered, for 5 minutes or until mixture boils and thickens.
6 Serve vegetable rolls with sauce; sprinkle with extra sesame seeds, if you like.

tips Bean curd sheets (also known as "yuba") are available from Asian food stores. If they are hard to find, use fresh rice noodle sheets or blanched cabbage leaves instead. Steam as the recipe directs.

VEGAN YOGURT

PREP + COOK TIME 5 MINUTES
(+ STANDING) MAKES 2½ CUPS

Place 1 cup cashews and 1 cup whole blanched
almonds in a large bowl; cover with cold water.
Stand, covered, for 4 hours or overnight. Drain;
rinse under cold water. Drain. Process nuts
with 1 cup water until it forms a yogurt-like
consistency.

PASSION FRUIT

STRAWBERRY

TIPS

You can experiment with different nuts to create this yogurt, bearing in mind the flavor each nut will create.

Stir in the juice of 1 lemon for a great savory yogurt option to add to salads or to top soups and curries.

Store vegan yogurt in the fridge for up to 1 week.

PASSION FRUIT

Make vegan yogurt on opposite page; stir in the pulp of 3 passion fruit.

STRAWBERRY

Make vegan yogurt on opposite page using 1 cup cashews and 1 cup pecans. Blend or process ½ pound strawberries until smooth. Fold strawberry purée through yogurt to create a swirled effect.

Zucchini & tofu noodles
WITH CILANTRO PESTO

PREP + COOK TIME 30 MINUTES **SERVES** 4

¼ cup olive oil

½ pound firm tofu, chopped coarsely

¾ pound zucchini, halved lengthwise, chopped coarsely

2 teaspoons finely grated fresh ginger

2 cloves garlic, crushed

1 tablespoon light soy sauce

6 ounces dried soba noodles

½ cup toasted cashews, chopped coarsely

1 cup loosely packed fresh cilantro leaves

CILANTRO PESTO

1 cup toasted cashews

3 cups loosely packed fresh cilantro leaves

1 clove garlic, crushed

2 teaspoons finely grated lemon zest

1 tablespoon lemon juice

1 fresh long green chile, seeded, chopped coarsely

½ cup olive oil

1 Make Cilantro Pesto.

2 Heat 2 tablespoons of the oil in a large deep frying pan over high heat; cook tofu for 3 minutes each side or until golden. Remove from pan; keep warm.

3 Heat remaining oil in same pan; cook squash and zucchini, stirring, for 5 minutes or until golden and tender. Add ginger and garlic; cook, stirring for 30 seconds or until fragrant. Add sauce; cook for 1 minute.

4 Meanwhile, cook noodles in a large saucepan of boiling water, uncovered, until just tender; drain. Return noodles to pan, add pesto; toss to combine.

5 Serve noodles with zucchini mixture and tofu; top with cashews and cilantro.

cilantro pesto Blend or process ingredients until smooth; season to taste.

tip You will need to buy 3 bunches of cilantro for this recipe.

Walnut & miso-filled
EGGPLANT WITH RADISH SALAD

PREP + COOK TIME 50 MINUTES SERVES 4

4 eggplants

2 tablespoons olive oil

½ cup finely chopped walnuts

½ cup cooked brown basmati rice

2 green onions, sliced thinly

1 clove garlic, crushed

1 tablespoon white miso paste

2 teaspoons light soy sauce

2 teaspoons mirin

RADISH SALAD

2 persian cucumbers, sliced thinly lengthwise

½ pound red radishes, trimmed, sliced thinly

2 green onions, sliced thinly lengthwise

2 tablespoons rice vinegar

2 teaspoons light soy sauce

¼ teaspoon sesame oil

1 Preheat oven to 350°F. Line a baking sheet with parchment paper.

2 Cut eggplants in half lengthwise. Score a ¼-inch border with a small knife. Spoon out flesh leaving a shell. Coarsely chop flesh. Place eggplant shells on baking sheet.

3 Heat oil in a non-stick large frying pan over high heat; cook chopped eggplant, walnuts, rice, green onions, and garlic, stirring, for 5 minutes or until eggplant is tender. Add miso, sauce, and mirin; cook, stirring, for 30 seconds or until eggplant is coated. Spoon mixture into eggplant shells.

4 Bake filled eggplant for 25 minutes or until golden and tender.

5 Meanwhile make Radish Salad.

6 Serve filled eggplants topped with radish salad.

radish salad Place ingredients in a medium bowl; toss gently to combine.

tip You can fill eggplants ahead of time; store, covered, in the refrigerator until required. Bake just before serving.

Chickpea "tofu" with SPICED BLACK-EYED PEAS

PREP + COOK TIME 1 HOUR 30 MINUTES (+ STANDING & REFRIGERATION) SERVES 4

You will need to start this recipe the day before.

¾ pound dried black-eyed peas

3 tablespoons olive oil

1 large yellow onion, chopped finely

4 cloves garlic, chopped finely

4 teaspoons finely grated fresh ginger

2 tablespoons ground cumin

1 tablespoon sweet paprika

½ teaspoon chili powder

1 can (14.5 oz) diced tomatoes

1 cup coconut cream

2 teaspoons superfine sugar

2 tablespoons lemon juice

⅓ cup chopped cashews, toasted, halved

1 fresh long green chile, sliced thinly

CHICKPEA "TOFU"

1 cup chickpea flour

2 teaspoons ground cumin

1 teaspoon ground turmeric

1 teaspoon flaky sea salt

3 cups water

1 Place dried peas in a medium bowl, cover with cold water; let stand 2 hours. Drain. Rinse under cold water; drain. Place peas in a medium saucepan of boiling water; return to a boil. Reduce heat; simmer, for 1 hour or until tender. Drain.

2 Meanwhile, make Chickpea "Tofu."

3 Heat 1 tablespoon of the oil in a large saucepan over medium heat; cook onion, garlic, ginger, cumin, paprika, and chili powder for 5 minutes or until onion softens. Add black-eyed peas, tomatoes, coconut cream, and sugar; cook, stirring occasionally, for 15 minutes or until sauce thickens. Stir in juice; season to taste.

4 Meanwhile, remove Chickpea "Tofu" from pan; cut into eight rectangles. Heat remaining 2 tablespoons oil in a large non-stick frying pan over high heat; cook Chickpea "Tofu" for 1 minute each side or until golden.

5 Serve Chickpea "Tofu" topped with bean mixture, cashews and chile.

chickpea "tofu" Grease and line a 8-inch square cake pan with parchment paper. Combine flour, cumin, turmeric and salt in a medium bowl. Add half the water; whisking, until smooth and combined. Place the remaining water in a medium saucepan over high heat; bring to a boil. Add chickpea mixture; cook, whisking continuously, for 2 minutes or until thick and glossy. Pour mixture into pan. Refrigerate for 2 hours or until set.

Miso vegetables with
POUNDED RICE SALAD

PREP + COOK TIME 30 MINUTES   SERVES 4

2 tablespoons sesame oil

4 king brown mushrooms, trimmed, quartered lengthwise

⅓ pound asparagus, trimmed, halved lengthwise

6 green onions, trimmed, sliced thinly

¾ pound enoki mushrooms, trimmed

POUNDED RICE SALAD

¼ cup sushi rice

1 large yellow bell pepper, sliced finely

1 large red bell pepper, sliced finely

½ cup loosely packed cilantro leaves

½ cup loosely packed mint leaves

1 cup mung bean sprouts

2 tablespoons sesame seeds, toasted

MISO SAUCE

¼ cup white (shiro) miso

¼ cup rice vinegar

1 tablespoon pure maple syrup

1 teaspoon finely chopped pickled ginger

1 tablespoon pickled ginger juice

½ teaspoon red pepper flakes

1 Make Pounded Rice Salad.

2 Make Miso Sauce.

3 Heat a wok over medium high heat. Add sesame oil and king brown mushrooms; stir-fry for 5 minutes. Transfer to a baking sheet. Stir-fry asparagus and green onions for 2 minutes; transfer to baking sheet. Stir-fry enoki mushrooms for 30 seconds or until heated through; transfer to baking sheet.

4 Serve vegetables topped with miso sauce and rice salad.

pounded rice salad Heat a large frying pan over medium heat, add rice; stir continuously for 4 minutes or until rice is lightly golden and toasted. Grind toasted rice in mortar and pestle to a fine powder. Place ground rice in a medium bowl with remaining ingredients; stir to combine.

miso sauce Whisk ingredients in a small bowl; season.

Broccolini & asparagus
WITH VEGAN YOGURT

PREP + COOK TIME 25 MINUTES **SERVES** 2

½ cup whole blanched almonds

1 teaspoon olive oil

1 teaspoon sweet paprika

⅓ pound broccolini, trimmed

¾ pound asparagus, trimmed

1½ ounces baby beet leaves (see tips)

½ cup fresh mint leaves

½ cup vegan yogurt (see page 210)

CHILE GARLIC DRESSING

¼ cup olive oil

1 fresh long red chile, seeded, sliced thinly

2 cloves garlic, sliced thinly

1 teaspoon finely chopped fresh ginger

1 teaspoon coriander seeds, crushed

2 tablespoons red wine vinegar

1 Preheat oven to 350°F. Line a baking sheet with parchment paper.

2 Place almonds on baking sheet; drizzle with oil and sprinkle with paprika. Toss to combine; season. Bake for 8 minutes or until golden; set aside to cool. Chop coarsely.

3 Meanwhile, make Chile Garlic Dressing.

4 Boil, steam or microwave broccolini and asparagus until tender; drain. Rinse under cold water; drain.

5 Serve broccolini and asparagus with beet leaves, mint, and chopped almonds; drizzle with dressing and dollop with yogurt.

chile garlic dressing Heat oil in a small frypan over low heat; cook chile, garlic, ginger, and seeds, stirring, 1 minute or until fragrant. Remove from heat; stir in vinegar.

tips You will need 1 bunch of broccolini and 2 bunches of asparagus for this recipe. Baby beet leaves are available from specialist green grocers and growers' markets. You can substitute with baby spinach leaves. You can prepare batches of paprika almonds and store them in an airtight container for up to 2 weeks. Add almonds to salads or eat them as a snack.

VEGGIES
with edible stalks

Broccoli The thicker stalks are also edible. Peel stalks with a vegetable peeler and cook slightly longer than the florets.

Cauliflower Treat the stalks in the same way you would broccoli.

Swiss chard The white stalks are the best bit. All they need is a slightly longer cooking time than the leaves to reveal their tender sweet taste.

PEPPERY WATERCRESS TOPS SUPERFOOD LISTS

Watercress contains a dense array of nutrients. It is high in vitamin K – a cup provides your requirements for the day. It's also terrific for eye health as it is rich in several carotenoids, has very good levels of several B-group vitamins, and among vegetables is a standout for calcium content. Both leaves and stems are edible although the stems tend to pack more of a mustardy-hot flavor punch. Think beyond salads and use in pestos or wilted with other greens.

WASTE NOT
want not

MONEY $AVER
USE BOTH THE STALKS AND STEMS OF VEGGIES

Salad days & ways

MISO + RICE WINE VINEGAR + unrefined sesame oil + orange zest + grated ginger = a yummy Asian dressing

COLD-PRESSED FLAXSEED OIL (high in omega-6 and -3) + extra-virgin olive oil + lemon juice & zest + dill + honey + crushed coriander seeds = an invigorating dressing for beans and shoots

Seeds are particularly rich in nutrients that are valuable for vegetarians. Make a seed mix for breakfast to be sprinkled over fruit or yogurt (dairy-based or vegan), and a seed mix for salads and savory dishes.

A DUKKAH OF SORTS

TURN A HALF-OPENED PACKAGE OF NUTS AND A FEW PANTRY SPICES INTO DUKKAH— THE WONDERFUL NORTH AFRICAN SPICE-AND-NUT MIXTURE. TOAST ANY KIND OF NUTS (EXCEPT PEANUTS), THEN CRUSH THEM WITH A MORTAR AND PESTLE. TOAST AND CRUSH CUMIN, CORIANDER, OR FENNEL SEEDS (ANY OR ALL OF THEM). COMBINE CRUSHED NUTS AND SPICES. DUKKAH IS DELICIOUS SPRINKLED ON PRACTICALLY EVERYTHING.

Ginger IS NICE IN...

Porridge with cinnamon and cardamom pods.

Steamed brown rice, pickled with apple cider vinegar, honey, and a little salt.

Roasted squash and bell pepper soup.

Try THESE *Raw*

ASPARAGUS Peel into thin strips with a vegetable peeler and toss with a lemony dressing and sliced chile.

BEET Grate, thinly shave, juice , or make a quick pickle, then pair with an apple or orange.

BROCCOLI Shave and toss with olive oil, honey, chopped preserved lemon, and coriander seeds.

BRUSSELS SPROUTS Shave and toss in a salad with pomegranate and sunflower seeds.

CAULIFLOWER Finely chop, shave , or quickly pickle.

CELERY ROOT Grate or cut into matchsticks, then combine with vegan mayonnaise; use as a side dish or sandwich filling.

KOHLRABI Grate or shave for a coleslaw.

Choco-cherry
COCONUT BARS

PREP + COOK TIME 30 MINUTES
(+ REFRIGERATION & FREEZING) MAKES 16

6 ounces dark (semi-sweet) vegan chocolate (see tip), chopped coarsely

1 cup dried cherries, chopped finely

3 cups desiccated coconut

½ cup rice malt syrup

1 teaspoon vanilla extract

⅓ cup melted coconut oil

1 Line base and sides of 7¼-inch x 11¼-inch slice pan with parchment paper.

2 Place half the chocolate in a small heatproof bowl over a saucepan of gently simmering water (don't allow bowl to touch water); stir until just melted. Pour chocolate into pan; spread to cover base. Refrigerate for 15 minutes or until set. Keep water at a gentle simmer; reserve bowl off the heat.

3 Combine cherries and coconut in a large bowl; stir in syrup, extract, and oil until combined. Press mixture very firmly in an even layer over chocolate.

4 Return pan of water to a gentle simmer over medium heat. Place remaining chocolate in reserved bowl over water; stir until melted. Pour chocolate over cherr- coconut layer; spread evenly with a spatula. Freeze for 1 hour or until set (alternatively, refrigerate for 3 hours or until set). Cut into bars before serving.

tip Vegan chocolate is available at health food stores.

Coconut fritters with MANGO, CHILE & LIME

PREP + COOK TIME 50 MINUTES SERVES 4

1 young coconut

2 medium bananas, mashed

¼ cup coconut cream

⅔ cup all-purpose flour

1 teaspoon baking powder

¾ cup shredded coconut

2½ tablespoons coconut nectar or agave syrup

rice bran oil, for deep-frying

2 tablespoons lime juice

1 mango, sliced thinly

1½ tablespoons finely grated lime zest

1 fresh long red chile, seeded, sliced thinly

1 Insert the tip of a small knife into the soft spot on the base of the coconut, using a twisting action. Place coconut over a glass; drain coconut water (reserve for another use). Wrap coconut in a clean towel, break open with a hammer, or by smashing it onto the floor. Spoon out the soft coconut flesh; you should have about ½ cup of the flesh. Thinly slice coconut flesh.

2 Combine fresh coconut, banana, coconut cream, ½ cup of the flour, baking powder, ¼ cup of the shredded coconut, and 2 teaspoons of the coconut nectar in a large bowl.

3 Combine remaining flour and shredded coconut in a medium bowl. Roll level tablespoons of coconut mixture into balls. Roll balls in flour mixture.

4 Fill a wok one-third with oil and heat to 325°F (or until a cube of bread browns in 25–30 seconds). Deep-fry coconut balls, in batches, for 2½ minutes or until golden and cooked through. Drain on paper towels.

5 Meanwhile, combine juice and remaining coconut nectar in a small bowl; stir in mango, zest, and chile.

6 Serve fritters with mango mixture and syrup.

Banoffee PIE

PREP + COOK TIME 40 MINUTES (+ REFRIGERATION) SERVES 8

You will need to start this recipe the day before.

¾ cup pecans

½ lb chocolate vegan cookies

½ cup coconut oil, at room temperature

1 tablespoon cacao powder

12 fresh dates, pitted

⅓ cup coconut sugar

1 tablespoon water

1 tablespoon cornstarch

1cup plus 2 tablespoons coconut cream

1 teaspoon vanilla extract

3 medium bananas

1 package (8 oz) silken tofu

2 tablespoons pure maple syrup

½ teaspoon ground cinnamon

1 Place pecans in a small bowl; cover with cold water. Let stand for 1 hour; drain.

2 Meanwhile, process cookies, coconut oil, cacao, and half the dates until fine crumbs form and mixture starts to clump. Press mixture over base and sides of a 9½-inch fluted tart tin. Refrigerate until required.

3 Stir coconut sugar and the water in a small saucepan over low heat until sugar dissolves. Bring to a boil; boil for 3 minutes or until mixture reduces slightly.

4 Meanwhile, whisk cornstarch and coconut cream in a small bowl. Gradually stir coconut cream mixture into sugar syrup until smooth; cook, stirring, for 10 minutes or until mixture boils and thickens.

5 Blend drained pecans and warm coconut mixture with remaining dates, extract, and 1 banana until as smooth as possible. Spoon mixture into cookie crust; smooth surface. Refrigerate overnight.

6 Blend or process tofu, syrup, and cinnamon until smooth.

7 Thinly slice remaining bananas; arrange slices on pie. Serve pie drizzled with tofu mixture.

tip If you have one, use a high-speed blender in step 5; this type of blender will produce a very smooth consistency.

Ginger, coconut & ALMOND BARS

PREP TIME 45 MINUTES (+ STANDING & REFRIGERATION) MAKES 16

You will need to start this recipe the day before.

1½ cups cashews

1 young coconut

1½ cups whole raw almonds

1 cup pitted dried dates, chopped coarsely

½ cup shredded coconut

¾ cup crystallized ginger, sliced thinly

¾ cup melted coconut oil

½ cup rice malt syrup

2 tablespoons finely grated fresh ginger

½ cup coconut milk

1½ teaspoons vanilla extract

2 tablespoons sliced almonds, toasted

1 Place cashews in a medium bowl; cover with cold water. Let stand for 1 hour; drain.

2 Line base and sides of a 9-inch square cake pan with parchment paper, extending the paper 2-inches over the sides.

3 Insert the tip of a small knife into the soft spot on the base of the coconut, using a twisting action. Place coconut over a glass; drain coconut water. (Reserve coconut water for another use). Wrap coconut in a clean towel, break open with a hammer, or by smashing it onto the floor. Spoon out the soft coconut flesh; you should have about ½ cup.

4 Process drained cashews and almonds until finely chopped. Add dates, shredded coconut, ¼ cup of the crystallized ginger, ¼ cup of the oil, and 1 tablespoon of the syrup; pulse until combined. Press mixture over base of pan. Refrigerate until required.

5 Blend or process fresh coconut, fresh ginger, coconut milk, extract, remaining oil, remaining syrup, and ¼ cup of the crystallized ginger until smooth. Pour mixture over date-nut base. Refrigerate overnight.

6 Cut into 16 bars; serve topped with sliced almonds and remaining crystallized ginger.

Raspberry ripple
CORN ICE CREAM

**PREP + COOK TIME 1 HOUR 30 MINUTES
(+ STANDING & FREEZING) MAKES 1 QUART**

This healthy non-dairy ice cream is made with corn, which provides a natural creaminess and sweetness. Expect the ice cream to be slightly more icy as a result.

2 trimmed ears of corn

2¼ cups coconut cream

2 cups unsweetened almond milk (see page 170)

¼ cup superfine sugar

2 teaspoons vanilla extract

½ cup agave syrup

1½ cups fresh or thawed frozen raspberries

CORNFLAKE CRUNCH

2 tablespoons superfine sugar

1 tablespoon agave syrup

1 tablespoon olive oil

½ teaspoon vanilla extract

2 cups cornflakes cereal

1 Using a sharp knife, cut kernels from cobs; reserve cobs. Place corn kernels, cobs, coconut cream, almond milk and sugar in a large saucepan over medium-high heat; bring to a boil. Reduce heat; simmer for 5 minutes or until corn is tender. Let stand for 1 hour.

2 Discard corn cobs. Blend or process corn mixture until smooth. Strain corn mixture; discard solids. Stir in extract and ⅓ cup of the agave syrup until combined.

3 Transfer corn mixture to an ice-cream machine. Churn mixture following manufacturer's instructions.

4 Meanwhile, blend or process raspberries with remaining agave syrup until smooth. Swirl raspberry mixture through almost frozen ice cream to create a ripple effect; pour into a 4-cup freezer-proof container. Freeze overnight or until firm.

5 Make Cornflake Crunch.

6 Serve ice cream topped with cornflake crunch.

cornflake crunch Preheat oven to 300°F. Line a baking sheet with parchment paper. Place sugar, agave syrup, oil, and extract in a small saucepan over low heat, stirring, until sugar dissolves. Place cornflakes in a medium bowl. Add syrup mixture; stir to combine. Spread cornflake mixture on baking sheet. Bake for 25 minutes or until slightly more golden. Leave to cool. Break into small pieces.

tips Take the ice cream out of the freezer 15 to 30 minutes before serving to soften it slightly. You could freeze the ice cream mixture into blocks and roll in cornflake crunch before serving.

GLOSSARY

AGAVE SYRUP from the agave plant; has a low GI, but that is due to the high percentage of fructose present, which may be harmful in large quantities.

ALLSPICE also known as pimento or jamaican pepper; so named because it tastes like a combination of nutmeg, cumin, clove, and cinnamon. Available whole or ground.

ALMONDS
blanched brown skins removed from the kernel.
ground also called almond meal; almonds are powdered to a coarse flour-like texture. **sliced** paper-thin slices.
sliced paper-thin slices.
slivered small pieces cut lengthwise.

BARLEY a nutritious grain used in soups and stews. Hulled barley, the least processed, is high in fiber. Pearl barley has had the husk removed then been steamed and polished so that only the "pearl" of the original grain remains, much the same as white rice.

BEANS
cannellini a small white bean similar in appearance and to other white beans (great northern, navy or haricot), all of which can be substituted for the other. Available dried or canned.
kidney medium-sized red bean, slightly floury in texture, yet sweet in flavor.

BEETS firm, round root vegetable.

BELL PEPPER Comes in many colors: red, green, yellow, orange and purplish-black. Be sure to discard seeds and membranes before use.

BAKING SODA a rising agent.

BREAD CRUMBS, PANKO (JAPANESE) are available in two varieties: larger pieces and fine crumbs. Both have a lighter texture than Western-style bread crumbs. They are available from Asian grocery stores and most supermarkets.

BRIOCHE French in origin; a rich, yeast-leavened, cake-like bread made with butter and eggs. Available from cake or specialty bread shops.

BROCCOLINI a cross between broccoli and chinese kale; it has long asparagus-like stems with a long loose floret, both are edible. Resembles broccoli but is milder and sweeter in taste.

BUTTER use salted or unsalted (sweet) butter; one stick of butter is equal to ½ cup.

BUTTERMILK originally the term given to the slightly sour liquid left after butter was churned from cream, today it is made from nonfat or low-fat milk to which specific bacterial cultures have been added. Despite its name, it is actually low in fat.

CARAWAY SEEDS the small, half-moon-shaped dried seed from a member of the parsley family; adds a sharp anise flavor in both sweet and savory dishes. Used widely, in foods such as rye bread, harissa and the classic Hungarian fresh cheese, liptauer.

CARDAMOM a spice native to India and used extensively in its cuisine; can be purchased in pod, seed, or ground form. Has a distinctive aromatic, sweetly rich flavor.

CELERY ROOT (CELERIAC) tuberous root with knobbly brown skin, white flesh and a celery-like flavor. Keep peeled celery root in acidulated water to stop it discoloring. It can be grated and eaten raw in salads; used in stews; mashed like potatoes; or sliced and deep-fried as chips.

CHAR SIU SAUCE a Chinese barbecue sauce made from sugar, water, salt, fermented soybean paste, honey, soy sauce, malt syrup, and spices. It can be found at most supermarkets.

CHEESE
feta Greek in origin; a crumbly textured goat- or sheep-milk cheese having a sharp, salty taste. Ripened and stored in salted whey.
goat made from goat's milk, has an earthy, strong taste; available in both soft and firm textures, in various shapes and sizes, and sometimes rolled in ash or herbs.
haloumi a firm, cream-colored sheep-milk cheese matured in brine; haloumi can be grilled or fried, briefly, without breaking down. Should be eaten while still warm as it becomes tough and rubbery on cooling.
manchego is a semi-firm Spanish sheep's milk cheese available from selected supermarkets or delis. You can use parmesan or pecorino cheese instead.
mozzarella soft, spun-curd cheese; originating in southern Italy where it was traditionally made from water-buffalo milk. Now generally made from cow's milk, it is the most popular pizza cheese because of its low melting point and elasticity when heated.
parmesan also called parmigiano; is a hard, grainy cow-milk cheese originating in Italy. Reggiano is the best variety.
pecorino the Italian generic name for cheeses made from sheep's milk; hard, white to pale-yellow in color. If you can't find it, use parmesan instead.
ricotta a soft, sweet, moist, white cow-milk cheese with a low fat content and a slightly grainy texture. The name roughly translates as "cooked again" and refers to ricotta's manufacture from a whey that is itself a by-product of other cheese making.

CHICKPEAS (GARBANZO BEANS) an irregularly round, sandy-colored legume. Has a firm texture even after cooking, a floury mouth-feel and robust nutty flavor; available canned or dried (soak for several hours in cold water before use).

CHILE generally, the smaller the chile, the hotter it is. Wear rubber gloves when seeding and chopping fresh chiles as they can burn your skin. Removing seeds and membranes lessens the heat level.
chipotle pronounced cheh-pote-lay. The name used for jalapeño chiles once they've been dried and smoked. With a deep, intensely smoky flavor, rather than a searing heat, chipotles are dark brown, almost black, and wrinkled in appearance.
jalapeño pronounced hah-lah-pain-yo. Fairly hot, medium-sized, plump, dark green chile; available pickled, sold canned or bottled, and fresh, from greengrocers.

CHINESE FIVE SPICE a fragrant mixture of ground cinnamon, cloves, star anise, sichuan pepper and fennel seeds. Available from most supermarkets or Asian food shops.

CILANTRO (CORIANDER) also known as pak chee or chinese parsley; a bright-green leafy herb with a pungent flavor. Both stems and roots of cilantro are also used in cooking; wash well before using. Also available ground or as seeds; these should not be substituted for fresh as the tastes are completely different.

CINNAMON available in pieces (called sticks) and ground into powder; one of the world's most common spices.

COCOA POWDER also called unsweetened cocoa; cocoa beans (cacao seeds) that have been fermented, roasted, shelled, ground into powder then cleared of most of the fat content.

COCONUT

cream obtained commercially from the first pressing of the coconut flesh alone, without the addition of water; the second pressing (less rich) is sold as coconut milk. Available in cans and cartons at most supermarkets.

desiccated concentrated, dried, unsweetened and finely shredded coconut flesh.

flaked dried flaked coconut flesh.

milk not the liquid inside the fruit (coconut water), but the diluted liquid from the second pressing of the white flesh of a mature coconut. Available in cans and cartons at most supermarkets.

oil is extracted from the coconut flesh so you don't get any of the fiber, protein, or carbohydrates present in the whole coconut. The best quality is virgin coconut oil, which is the oil pressed from the dried coconut flesh, and doesn't include the use of solvents or other refining processes.

shredded thin strips of dried coconut.

sugar is not made from coconuts, but the sap of the blossoms of the coconut palm tree. The refined sap looks a little like raw or light brown sugar, and has a similar caramel flavor. It also has the same amount of calories as regular white (granulated) sugar.

CORNSTARCH available made from corn or wheat (wheaten cornstarch, gluten-free, gives a lighter texture in cakes); used as a thickening agent in cooking.

CREAM also called pure or fresh cream. It has no additives and contains a minimum fat content of 35%.

CUMIN also known as zeera or comino; has a spicy, nutty flavor.

EGGPLANT also known as aubergine.

FENNEL also known as finocchio or anise; a white to very pale green-white, firm, crisp, roundish vegetable about 3–5 inches in diameter. The bulb has a slightly sweet, anise flavor but the leaves have a much stronger taste. Also the name of dried seeds having a licorice flavor.

FISH FILLETS, FIRM WHITE blue eye, bream, flathead, snapper, ling, swordfish, whiting, jewfish, or sea perch are all good choices. Check for small pieces of bone and use tweezers to remove them.

FISH SAUCE also called nam pla or nuoc nam; made from pulverised salted fermented fish, most often anchovies. Has a pungent smell and strong taste, so use sparingly.

FLOUR

all-purpose (plain) a general all-purpose wheat flour.

chickpea (besan) creamy yellow flour made from chickpeas and is very nutritious.

rice very fine, almost powdery, gluten-free flour; made from ground white rice. Used in baking, as a thickener, and in some Asian noodles and desserts. Another variety, made from glutinous sweet rice, is used for chinese dumplings and rice paper.

self-rising all-purpose flour sifted with baking powder in the proportion of 1 cup flour to 2 teaspoons baking powder.

GAI LAN also known as chinese broccoli, gai larn, kanah, gai lum and chinese kale; used more for its stems than its coarse leaves.

GINGER, PICKLED pink or red in color, paper-thin shavings of ginger pickled in a mixture of vinegar, sugar, and natural coloring. Available from Asian food shops.

HARISSA a Moroccan paste made from dried chiles, cumin, garlic, oil, and caraway seeds. Available from Middle Eastern food shops and supermarkets.

HOISIN SAUCE a thick, sweet and spicy Chinese paste made from salted fermented soy beans, onions, and garlic.

HORSERADISH CREAM is a commercially prepared creamy paste consisting of grated horseradish, vinegar, oil, and sugar.

KAFFIR LIME LEAVES also known as bai magrood. Aromatic leaves of a citrus tree; two glossy dark green leaves joined end to end, forming a rounded hourglass shape. A strip of fresh lime peel may be substituted for each kaffir lime leaf.

KECAP MANIS a thick soy sauce with added sugar and spices. The sweetness comes from the addition of molasses or palm sugar.

LSA A ground mixture of linseeds (L; also called flaxseeds), sunflower seeds (S), and almonds (A); available from supermarkets and health-food stores.

LEMONGRASS a tall, clumping, lemon-smelling and -tasting, sharp-edged grass; the white part of the stem is used, finely chopped, in cooking.

LENTILS (red, brown, yellow) dried pulses often identified by and named after their color; also known as dhal.

MAPLE SYRUP, PURE distilled from the sap of sugar maple trees found only in Canada and the USA. Maple-flavored syrup or pancake syrup is not an adequate substitute for the real thing.

MIRIN a Japanese champagne-colored cooking wine; made of glutinous rice and alcohol and used expressly for cooking. Should not be confused with sake.

MUSHROOMS

cremini also known as swiss brown or roman mushrooms; are light brown mushrooms with a full-bodied flavor.

enoki have clumps of long, spaghetti-like stems with tiny, snowy white caps.

oyster also called abalone; grey-white mushroom shaped like a fan. Prized for their smooth texture and subtle, oyster-like flavor.

porcini also known as cèpes; the richest-flavored mushrooms. Expensive, but because they're so strongly flavored, only a small amount is required.

portobello are mature, fully opened creminis; they are larger and bigger in flavor.

shiitake, fresh also known as chinese black, forest, or golden oak mushrooms; although cultivated, they are large and meaty and have the earthiness and taste of wild mushrooms.

NAPA CABBAGE also known as peking or chinese cabbage. Elongated in shape with pale green, crinkly leaves.

OIL

coconut see Coconut

cooking spray we use a cooking spray made from canola oil.

olive made from ripened olives. Extra-virgin and virgin are the first and second press, respectively, of the olives; "light" refers to taste, not fat levels.

peanut pressed from ground peanuts; most commonly used oil in Asian cooking because of its high smoke point (capacity to handle high heat without burning).

sesame used as a flavoring rather than a cooking medium.

ONIONS, GREEN (SCALLIONS) also called, incorrectly, shallot; an immature onion picked before the bulb has formed. Has a long, bright-green edible stalk.

PAPRIKA ground, dried, sweet red bell pepper; there are many types available, including sweet, hot, mild, and smoked.

PARCHMENT PAPER also called baking paper or baking parchment—is a silicone-coated paper that is primarily used for lining baking pans and baking sheets so cooked food doesn't stick, making removal easy.

POLENTA also known as cornmeal; a flour-like cereal made of ground corn (maize). Also the name of the dish made from it.

POMEGRANATE dark-red, leathery-skinned fruit about the size of an orange filled with hundreds of seeds, each wrapped in an edible lucent-crimson pulp with a unique tangy sweet-sour flavor.

POMEGRANATE MOLASSES not to be confused with pomegranate syrup or grenadine; pomegranate molasses is thicker, browner and more concentrated in flavor—tart, sharp, slightly sweet and fruity. Available from Middle Eastern food shops or specialty food shops, and some supermarkets.

PRESERVED LEMON RIND a North African specialty; lemons are quartered and preserved in salt and lemon juice or water. To use, remove and discard pulp, squeeze juice from rind, rinse rind well; slice thinly. Once opened, store under refrigeration.

PROSCIUTTO unsmoked italian ham; salted, air-cured, and aged.

QUINOA pronounced keen-wa; is a gluten-free grain. It has a delicate, slightly nutty taste and chewy texture.

RICE MALT SYRUP also known as brown rice syrup or rice syrup; is made by cooking brown rice flour with enzymes to break down its starch into sugars from which the water is removed.

SAFFRON available ground or in strands; imparts a yellow-orange color to food once infused. The quality can vary greatly; the best is the most expensive spice in the world.

SEMOLINA coarsely ground flour milled from durum wheat; the flour used in making gnocchi, pasta, and couscous.

SWISS CHARD also called swiss chard; mistakenly called spinach.

SOY SAUCE made from fermented soybeans. Several variations are available in most supermarkets and Asian food stores. We use japanese soy sauce unless stated otherwise.

SPINACH also known as english spinach and, incorrectly, swiss chard.

SRIRACHA a medium-hot chile sauce available from Asian food stores and supermarkets.

SUGAR

brown very soft, finely granulated sugar retaining molasses for its characteristic color and flavor.

coconut see Coconut

palm also called nam tan pip, jaggery, jawa, or gula melaka; made from the sap of the sugar palm tree. Light brown to black in color and usually sold in rock-hard cakes; use brown sugar if unavailable.

raw natural brown granulated sugar.

superfine (caster) finely granulated table sugar.

SUMAC a purple-red, astringent spice ground from berries growing on shrubs flourishing wild around the Mediterranean; adds a tart, lemony flavor to food. Available from major supermarkets.

SWEET POTATO (KUMARA) the Polynesian name of an orange-fleshed sweet potato often confused with yam.

TAHINI a rich, sesame-seed paste.

TAMARI a thick, dark soy sauce made mainly from soybeans, but without the wheat used in most standard soy sauces.

TOASTING/ROASTING desiccated coconut, pine nuts and sesame seeds toast more evenly if stirred over low heat in a heavy-bottomed frying pan; their natural oils will help turn them golden brown. Remove from pan immediately. Nuts and dried coconut can be toasted in the oven to release their aromatic essential oils. Spread them evenly onto a baking sheet, then toast at 350°F for about 5 minutes.

TOFU also called bean curd; an off-white, custard-like product made from the "milk" of crushed soybeans. Comes fresh as soft or firm, and processed as fried or pressed dried sheets. Fresh tofu can be refrigerated in water (changed daily) for up to 4 days.

WATERCRESS one of the cress family, a large group of peppery greens. Highly perishable, so must be used as soon as possible after purchase. It has an exceptionally high vitamin K content, which is great for eye health, and is an excellent source of calcium.

WHITE MISO (SHIRO) Japan's famous bean paste made from fermented soybeans and rice, rye or barley. It varies in color, texture, and saltiness. Available from supermarkets.

WRAPPERS, GOW GEE made of flour, egg, and water; are found in the refrigerated or freezer section of Asian food shops and supermarkets. These come in different thicknesses and shapes.

YEAST (dried and fresh), a rising agent used in dough making. Granular and fresh compressed (blocks) yeast can almost always be substituted for the other.

YOGURT, GREEK-STYLE plain yogurt strained in a cloth (muslin) to remove the whey and to give it a creamy consistency.

Index

weldon**owen**

Published in North America by Weldon Owen
1045 Sansome Street, San Francisco, CA 94111
www.weldonowen.com
Weldon Owen is a division of Bonnier Publishing USA

This edition published in arrangement with Bauer Media Pty Limited. First
published in Australia in 2017 by Bauer Media Pty Limited under the title
Almost Vegetarian. © Bauer Media Pty Limited 2017. All rights reserved.

ISBN 978-1-68188-377-9

Library of Congress Cataloging-in-Publication data is available

Printed and bound in China

This edition printed in 2017

10 9 8 7 6 5 4 3 2 1